MARVEL CINEMATIC UNIVERSE: MOVIE MISTAKES & TRIVIA

Jon Sandys

Thanks to oswal13, Casual Person, Phaneron, GalahadFairlight, Sacha, Sammo, Bishop73, Friso94, TedStixon, wizard_of_gore, Rydersriot87, THGhost, ployp, jimba, Tricia Webster, SheWhoLovesMovies, MFWills, hooksfan, Daniel4646, Jedd Jong, zev, Cubs Fan, Super Grover, Guy, Comedyfan74, Brad, Blathrop, Quantom X, PEDAUNT, oddy knocky, Charles Austin Miller, Nik Rolls, Erik M., MasterOfAll, Kane A R, BocaDavie, Sweeney7odd, lionhead, dablues7, erwin, Stefan Nygren, James Thomas, Jay Mallone, HulkObsessedChick, Epic, clbowen1, monsa, CCARNI, jesus32567, Gpepsi, Velganice, David R. Akens, Kit Sullivan, Nitram1967, carguy4u2always, GillBill, MJ 85, FleetCommand, gazza2009, MikeH, AD, P Michael Reed, jaydowg23, Stephen Warouw, buzzed, rasmioche, LizzieWD, Donatello, greydane, NuclearNemesis, grgmssgnn, ComicBoy, Fat Tony69, Scorpious, Danpoole, Icegirl, thisisjl, n_frisby, Quinny, Carol Sardinha, The First Avenger, Jennyred, Kaison Vourne, jaarons, Arokthis, shadowgirl, Teru_Kage, firexcpro, Joseph M Vazquez, Phixius, Keith Barak Chan, mystiemyth, johnrosa, and all the anonymous submitters who helped make this book, and moviemistakes.com, what they are.

Thank you for buying this book! I hope you enjoy it, and if so please tell your friends, share it, lend it...spread the word! I'd love to hear any suggestions, corrections, thoughts and opinions - please get in touch at jon@moviemistakes.com. And please leave a review on Amazon - if you like this, there's plenty more where this came from. And if you've got any observations of your own, please submit them to moviemistakes.com and let other people know about them!

CONTENTS

A NOTE ABOUT TIMES

Lots of the entries here have times after them, to help find them when watching. Due to the nature of different releases, and especially the difference between formats, the times might be approximate. For example NTSC (used in the US) and PAL (used in lots of other places) mean times can be off by 4% (to do with frame rates - I won't bore you with the technical side here, but Google will help you out if you're keen!). So if you're trying to find something and the time doesn't seem quite right, go forwards/back a bit and you should find the relevant scene.

IRON MAN MISTAKES

When Iron Man and Iron Monger are fighting, Iron Man catches the SUV, and you can see the family inside the car. Although the car is completely vertical, the hair of the people in the car seems to defy gravity.

When Pepper is watching the television program about Stark Industries' stock troubles, after Tony's press conference, notice she has a wireless headset in her left ear. When Tony calls her down to the lab, the camera flashes back to Pepper and the ear piece is gone. (00:48:50)

Paramount Pictures

In the extra footage after the credits, the reflection of the crew is visible in the picture frames around the apartment.

Paramount Pictures

After flight testing the suit the first time, Tony crashes through his house, landing on and partly crushing his blue Cobra roadster, as building debris litters the ground around and on the car. Later, when Pepper finds Tony being fitted by robotic arms, we see the same garage area in the background and the Cobra and debris have been cleared away, replaced by the 1932 Ford hot rod. Still later, when Tony suits up for the final battle, the damaged Cobra and all the debris is back in place in time for him to shove the car out of the way. Note the same location in all three shots is below the second set of windows on the wall. (01:04:30 - 01:42:15)

When Stark is paralysed his fringe (hair bangs) keeps changing style all the time.

When we first see Tony Stark arrive at the benefit, his car doesn't have a front plate. When we actually see him pull up to the entrance though, his personalised "Stark" plate has appeared.

Paramount Pictures

When Tony Stark is at home he's wearing a black tank top while working on the suit, and there is a bad cover-up of one of his tattoos. It almost looks like a band-aid is over it. It goes away and comes back.

When Stark fires the two rockets to Raza, before Yinsen dies, there are two green rockets standing next to him that change position in less than a second.

When Tony is paralysed on the couch, in one shot his head is facing to the left. However, in the very next shot he is facing forward and slightly slouching back a bit. There wasn't enough time for him to move into the other position, even if he wasn't paralysed.

After Stark is paralysed and slightly recovers, he goes to get his energy. Right then the blood around his left ear has vanished. Being seconds away from dying, the last thing he would think of is taking a shower.

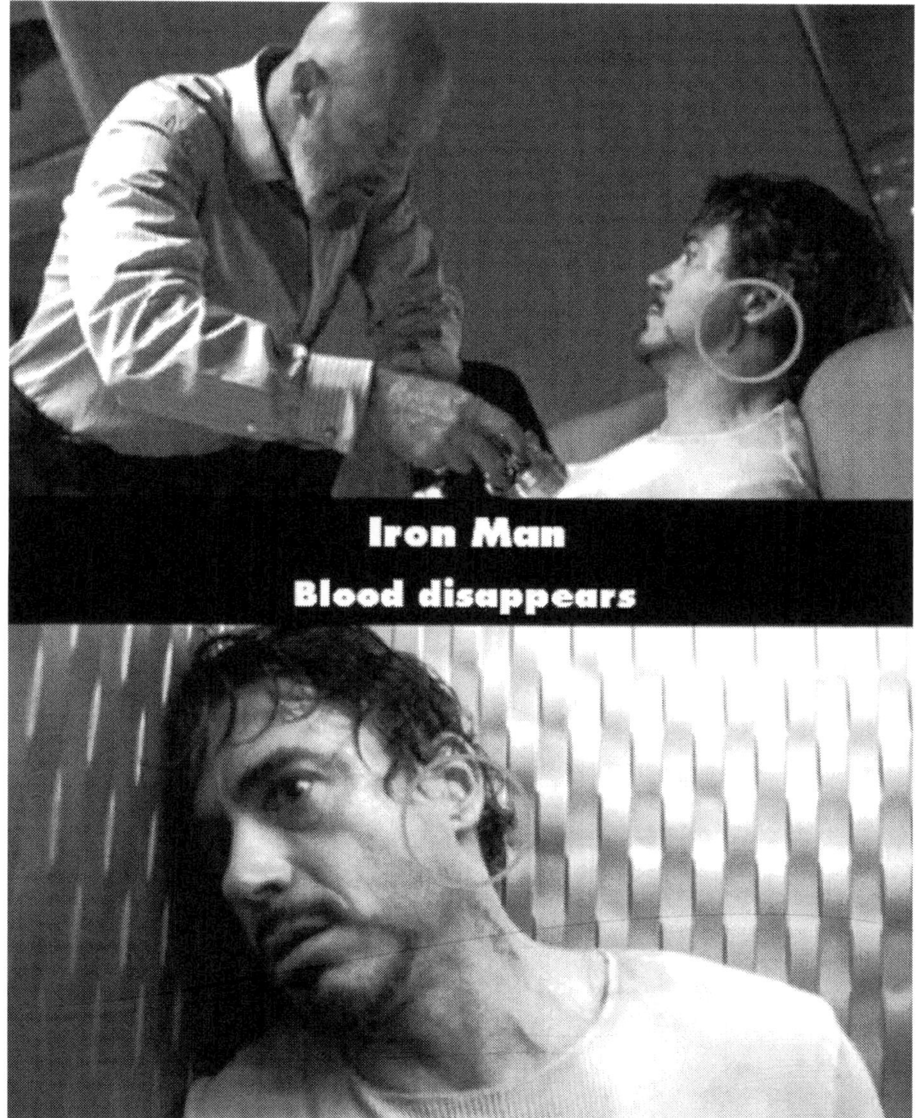

Paramount Pictures

Just after Pepper replaces Tony's chest piece, she clenches her hands, complaining about how disgusting the "pus" is. When the shot changes, she closes her hand again.

When Tony's convoy was ambushed at the beginning of the movie he was riding in an non-armored HMMWV. Prior to 2007, all vehicles that leave the base are uparmored in Iraq and Afghanistan, under no circumstances do you leave base in a soft vehicle. The Airmen were wearing the Airman Battle Uniform, which was released for use in the Middle East around 2007, so the movie couldn't have taken place prior to that time period. Some people may try to correct this by claiming that the military doesn't have enough uparmored vehicles to go around and they just got the short end of the stick. That is not the case today like it was a few years ago. Even if it was the case, the military wouldn't put a passenger who would be considered a "high value target" to the enemy like Tony at risk for capture or death in a soft vehicle, especially with his knowledge of weapon systems that can be used against the US.

When Iron Man catches the Audi SUV, the front wings/fenders don't bend when he catches it, the car weighs close to 2 tons, some damage should occur to them as they are made of such thin metal.

Some of the shots involving the terrorists firing at the prototype suit are "flipped" duplicates of other shots. In the scene where he first emerges from the cave, several of the terrorists are firing M4-type rifles with the ejection port on the LEFT side of the rifle. In reality, except for a few specially made versions, all M4-types eject spent brass through an ejection port on the right. Later in the scene, this shot is repeated, but with the proper orientation.

In the montage of Stark designing the Mark II suit on his computer, he picks up a coffee mug to his left and absent-mindedly drinks it, then gets a not-good expression as the liquid was presumably not what he was expecting. A second earlier, the coffee mug had been shown completely upside-down on the desk.

Paramount Pictures

After Stark escapes, he is walking in the desert, and crests the brow of a sand dune. Then, helicopters burst into view over him and you hear them for the first time. Stark was on the brow of the dune and should have heard them long before.

When the "Jericho" rocket explodes in the distance, an explosion is heard simultaneously, this is not possible due to the speed of sound being much slower than the speed of light.

There is a misspelling on the cover of the issue of Forbes magazine shown in the presentation about Stark's life. It reads "Tony Stark takes reigns at 21". The correct spelling of the word is "reins". Stark may "reign" at Stark Industries but he would take over the "reins" of the company.

Paramount Pictures

After Tony demonstrates the Jericho for the first time, the aftershock hits the soldiers in the face and blows at least three people's hats off. From the side shot of the event, happening simultaneously, you can only see one hat being blown into the air. The aftershock also makes a dead stop, weakening too quickly and appearing anti-climactic. The aftershock should have blown at least ten yards more before dying out.

When Pepper runs out of the Stark Industries building and says "Obadiah, he's gone insane", her lips don't match with her mouth.

IRON MAN TRIVIA

Notice they don't play the lyrics with the "Iron Man" song in the closing credits. That's because the Black Sabbath song was not about the comic book Iron Man. There are many theories about what the song means, but the most popular is that it is about a man who travels to the future and sees the apocalypse. They couldn't use the lyrics to describe the Iron Man in the movie: He was turned to steel - In the great magnetic field - Where he traveled time - For the future of mankind. Now the time is here - For Iron Man to spread fear - Vengeance from the grave - Kills the people he once saved.

The first terrorist to be killed by Iron Man is Tom Morello, the guitarist in Rage Against the Machine and Audioslave. Audioslave's song "Cochise" was used in previews.

Paramount Pictures

The lead terrorist gives a speech about Genghis Khan's use of the bow and arrow. Iron Man's archenemy in the comics, The Mandarin, claims to be a direct descendant of Genghis Khan.

Stan Lee makes his usual cameo, this time seen as a man who Tony Stark mistakes as Hugh Hefner.

Paramount Pictures

The theme song from the Iron Man (1966) cartoon series is played in several shots. In the casino scene, in Stark's bedroom scene, and finally it is the personalized ringtone for Stark on James Rhodes' cellphone.

The name of the terrorist group that abducts Tony, "The Ten Rings," is a reference to an infamous Iron Man villain, "The Mandarin," who possessed 10 magical rings.

In the movie, Jarvis is Tony's automated system. In the comics, Jarvis is the name of his butler, who later becomes the butler for the Avengers.

Director Jon Favreau appears as Happy Hogan, one of Tony's personal assistants.

While on the plane, there is a video featuring Ghostface Killah (of the Wu-Tang Clan), whose alias is Tony Stark.

When Pepper Potts is stealing Obediah's files off of Tony Stark's computer in his office, pay close attention to some of the names of the files. On several files that show on the computer screen, a few are labeled "Lebowski". A playful homage to Jeff Bridges (who plays Obediah) and his famous slacker character from the movie of the same name.

The movie has some interesting hidden promises: Downey will appear in *The Incredible Hulk* (again as Iron Man), while at this movie's conclusion, the Avengers are mentioned. Thus, whereas the previous Marvel features (*X-Men, Daredevil, Spider-Man*) were essentially stand-alones, the *Iron Man* movie initiates the first character crossovers in the Marvel Comics movie conversions.

The reason Stark's friend Rhodes looks at the suit of armor at the end of the movie and says something like "Next Time!" is because in the comic books he ends up actually having his own suit of armor, donning the name War Machine, as later happened in the MCU. He backs Tony Stark up in many situations and is one of his most trusted friends.

After Tony's press conference about stopping Stark Industries weapons manufacturing, Obidiah Stane uses the phrase "Iron Monger". This is the name given to his character in the comics, when he dons the suit seen at the end of the movie.

Stay until after the credits where there is a scene with Samuel Jackson playing a certain eye-patched head of SHIELD.

Near the end of the movie, Stark's alibi from the SHIELD agent calls Iron Man Stark's bodyguard. In the early comics the public believed Iron Man was Stark's bodyguard.

Tony Stark's final line in the film is, "I am Iron Man." This is the opening line to the song "Iron Man" by Black Sabbath, which immediately follows. It is mentioned in the novelization that this was intentional, as "Iron Man" was one of Stark's favorite songs.

In the scene where Col. James Rhodes briefs the media about the "training exercise" incident, if you look at the microphones at the podium, you can see three from left to right, 10 News, 19 KJFM and 6 KPGB. The first two are facing flat revealing the numbers 10 and 19, and the 3rd is at an angle so you can see the 6 twice, making 10-19-66 or October 19, 1966, the director Jon Favreau's birthday.

During the first part of the end credits we see a simple animation that eventually resolves itself into the symbol of SHIELD. Part of this animation shows not the Iron Man, but the War Machine armor (note the shoulder-mounted external machine gun, for example) that Tony Stark constructed for James Rhodes in the comic book. This is the second hint in the movie at Rhodes becoming War Machine in the future (the first being Rhodes glancing at an unfinished armor and saying, "Next time").

The call sign of the lead F-22 Raptor pilot is "Whiplash One". Whiplash is the name of the main villain in Iron Man 2.

Marvel's Kevin Feige has confirmed that Captain America's shield is indeed visible in the workshop scene (when Pepper asks Tony, "Are those bullet holes?"), a subtle nod to Marvel's Captain America movie set for 2011.

THE INCREDIBLE HULK MISTAKES

When Dr. Ross and Bruce are in the hotel room, Banner empties the purse on the bed and there is some cash inside the wallet. As they are about to leave he picks up the cash, which isn't in the wallet anymore.(01:08:10)

Universal Pictures

In the motel room, Betty gives Bruce a new heart monitor watch, still in its box. In a subsequent shot, the box has disappeared and Bruce is putting the watch on. The cut to Betty and back is too fast for him to have taken the watch out and junked the box. (01:04:10)

Universal Pictures

During the street chase in Brazil, the time of day changes from night, to perhaps late afternoon/evening, to night again.

When the Hulk walks through the stream, the water doesn't react to his feet. (00:59:20)

At the beginning of the movie, when the general wears his dress greens, his epaulet rank has the stripe near his neck. Later,in a shot about halfway through, the stripe is near his shoulder.

During the opening credits, the camera approaches Betty's bed, where she lies unconscious. The first shot shows her head straight, but an immediate closer angle shows it tilted to the left.

As Emil is in the men's restroom looking at the mirror, some of his hair is hanging over his forehead, but when the shot changes, his hair is suddenly brushed back.

You have to be quick to spot this one, but when Bruce is ringing the bell on his bike, you see a woman on her mobile phone for about a second, in the next shot it has disappeared.

When Bruce and Betty are hugging on the bridge, they turn back and forth about a quarter of a turn whenever the camera angle changes.

When the police are searching for abomination in New York City, they reach an alleyway where there's a police car marked 'Toronto Police'.

When Hulk throws the chunk of sheet metal at the helicopter, it glances off the rotor housing (taking a ragged piece with it.) When the chopper crashes, however, the propeller comes off with a perfectly clean edge, as if the projectile had sheared completely through the base.

In the scene where Betty drives up behind Bruce in her car as he begins to cross the bridge, Bruce's left hand is visibly clutching his jacket shut. In the next shot from inside Betty's car, his hand is immediately at his side. (00:42:20)

The USB drive should have been destroyed after sitting in Bruce's stomach for a day, or at least been somewhere in his intestines, so he wouldn't have been able to puke it up.

After the first time we see Bruce transform into the Hulk, he has hitched a ride with the elderly man. You will remember he has 3 1/4 length pants on with a few rips. It cuts to a quick clip of him walking up the road but this time he has full length pants on. They switch back to shorter length pants straight after.

Bruce is seen wearing a Polar F5 heart rate monitor in a couple of scenes after Betty gives it to him (such as when he is in bed with Betty) but there is no transmitter strap around his chest, which that model needs in order to pick up the wearer's heart rate.

At one point during the final battle, Betty puts her hand on the minigun. Having been recently fired for long periods, that thing would be scalding hot and would badly burn her hand.

When Dr. Ross empties her handbag on the bed, there is a Givenchy compact with the Givenchy insignia face up. When the bed is shown again, the compact is face down.

In the beginning of the film, Bruce Banner's hair is a dark brown and looks natural. When he is doing the anger control exercises, he is obviously wearing a black wig which is not natural looking at all. This happens a few times during the movie - it switches from his natural hair to the very dark wig. And at times, even his eyebrows look much darker and thicker.

Near the start of the movie, in Brazil, Bruce is studying Portuguese but the people are speaking Spanish. Brazilians speak Portuguese.

When Blonsky is seen wearing the American Class A uniform,

it's visible he has not shaved his face for days. Quite unthinkable for the military - be it American or British. If he had time to change from his BDUs to the Class A uniform then he would have had time to shave as well. Soldiers in Iraq aren't even excused from shaving daily unless they have a medical condition that prevents them from shaving.

THE INCREDIBLE HULK TRIVIA

Paul Soles, who portrays the character Stanley, was the voice of Dr. Bruce Banner for the 1966 cartoon of The Incredible Hulk. The name "Stanley" is itself likely a reference to Hulk co-creator Stan Lee.

When General Ross is drinking at the bar, his drink is made up of equal parts of Hennessy, Cognac and Hypnotiq liqueur. The name for this drink is an "Incredible Hulk."

At one point in the movie, when Bruce is walking on the streets at night, a song which has been popularly called Lonely Man is heard playing. This is the same song that was used at the end of every episode of the TV series The Incredible Hulk which starred Bill Bixby and Lou Ferrigno.

Originally, the only line the Hulk was going to have was saying Betty's name. However, Letterier noticed that fans wanted the Hulk to have more lines so he added "Leave me alone" and "Hulk Smash."

In the opening credits, a list of names is seen as being Bruce's known associates. One of the names is Rick Jones. In *The Incredible Hulk* comics, Rick Jones drove out onto the weapons testing site on a dare. Bruce saved his life, but that sacrifice caused Bruce to become the Hulk.

At the start of the movie, Banner is watching TV, and a man gets slapped across the face. This is a young Bill Bixby who went on to play Banner in The Incredible Hulk TV Series.

When Bruce is browsing through Betty Ross's files, we can briefly glimpse a file name with something to the effect of "animal webbing in human subjects". A nod to Spider-Man, perhaps?

The news clip mentioned a campus magazine reporter called Jack McGee who had witnessed the Hulk assault in the grounds. This is a nod to the TV series where David Banner was pursued by an investigative reporter of the same name.

During the creation of Abomination, the doctor performing the procedure gets some infected blood in a cut on his head and his head starts to pulsate. This looks like it will be a set up for the Leader to appear. The Leader is a character with enhanced brain power but ordinary strength.

Stan Lee (Stanley Martin Lieber), the original creator of this comic book hero, has his usual cameo role in this movie. He's the guy who drinks the gamma contaminated soda from the fridge.

Universal Pictures

In the film, a serum is mentioned as being created during World

War II. This is a reference to the super soldier serum that created Captain America.

The green cross, projected onto Dr. Banner's forehead, is exactly the same as the one from the original TV series.

Not only is STARK industries used, i.e. *Iron Man,* but Nick Fury, another Marvel hero, is mentioned on a piece of paper. Nick Fury is played by Samuel L. Jackson in Iron Man, so maybe another hint at Avengers, as Nick Fury is an agent of SHIELD.

The security guard Banner manages to bribe with pizza is Lou Ferrigno, who played the Hulk in the TV series. Ferrigno also had a cameo as a security guard in The Hulk (2003).

In the scene in the hotel Betty throws Bruce a pair of large purple shorts she has bought. This is a nod to the comic where the Hulk always wore large purple shorts.

In addition to the large purple stretchy shorts already mentioned, Betty came back with a lumberjack style shirt, which she put on herself - a nod to the TV series where David Banner often wore one of these ahead of the rip scenes.

Aside from Lou Ferrigno appearing in the film, there are other nods to the TV series such as the piano song about 1/4 of the way through the film(when Dr Banner is walking the streets) and when Dr Banner and Dr Ross steal the truck, it's a 70's model F-150 which Dr Banner also drove in the TV series, albeit a different colored one.

When Bruce receives Betty's necklace in the mail, the package is addressed to David B. The name David Banner was used in the The Incredible Hulk TV series when it was decided the name Bruce would lead people to think the character was homosexual.

Near the end of the film, Bruce Banner falls from a helicopter, transforming into the Hulk just before hitting the ground. This is a reversal of a scene from the TV movie "The Death of the Incredible Hulk" in which the Hulk falls from an airplane, transforming back into Banner just before hitting the ground.

When the two soldiers try to fight the Abomination, they find a rocket launcher in a case. This launcher is actually a painted Nerf-toy. Nerf later released it again in a green and silver scheme as a tie-in with this movie.

IRON MAN 2 MISTAKES

In the final scene when Stark, Rhodes and the senator have a picture taken, Tony's jacket is first buttoned, then unbuttoned from the same viewing angle. (01:56:50)

At the end of the movie where Stark, Rhody and the Senator are taking a photo, Stark's hand is supposed to be behind the senator but when the scene switches to the zoomed out view, his hands are by his side and when it switches back again, his hands are behind the senator.

In the scene where Mickey Rourke is in the laboratory discussing how long it will take him to reproduce the robots, his glasses change position from him wearing them to not wearing them throughout the conversation.

When Tony goes to the bathroom and scans his blood toxicity, the Tony who faces the camera is supposed to be his reflection in the mirror, but oddly the problem is the reflection is not actually reversed. And note how he scanned his right hand's finger, but then he's sucking on his left hand's pricked finger. (00:28:30)

When Ivan climbs the ladder to inspect the Hammer prototype, his hair changes repeatedly from underneath the frames of his glasses to outside the frames. (00:51:00)

Paramount Studios

Rhodey falls on the brook far from the cascade. When he stands up he is now standing much closer to the cascade.

In the scene where Whiplash is talking on the phone with Tony, you can see fresh blood running down his hand, but when it goes to the close up of him, the blood is wiped off and there is only a stain. (01:31:00)

Paramount Studios

While Rhodey and Stark are fighting, right before the house explodes, all the guests run away. Half a second later an aerial view shows the house being blown to pieces, but not a single person or car is seen on the premises.

In Monaco, Stark smashes his head against a green car. When he falls on the ground there's a red sign with the numbers 885 on it. In further shots the sign has disappeared.

When Mickey Rourke puts the explosive onto the wall, he slaps it down and it spreads out a bit. We cut to a quick closer shot, and it's suddenly more compacted. (00:43:25)

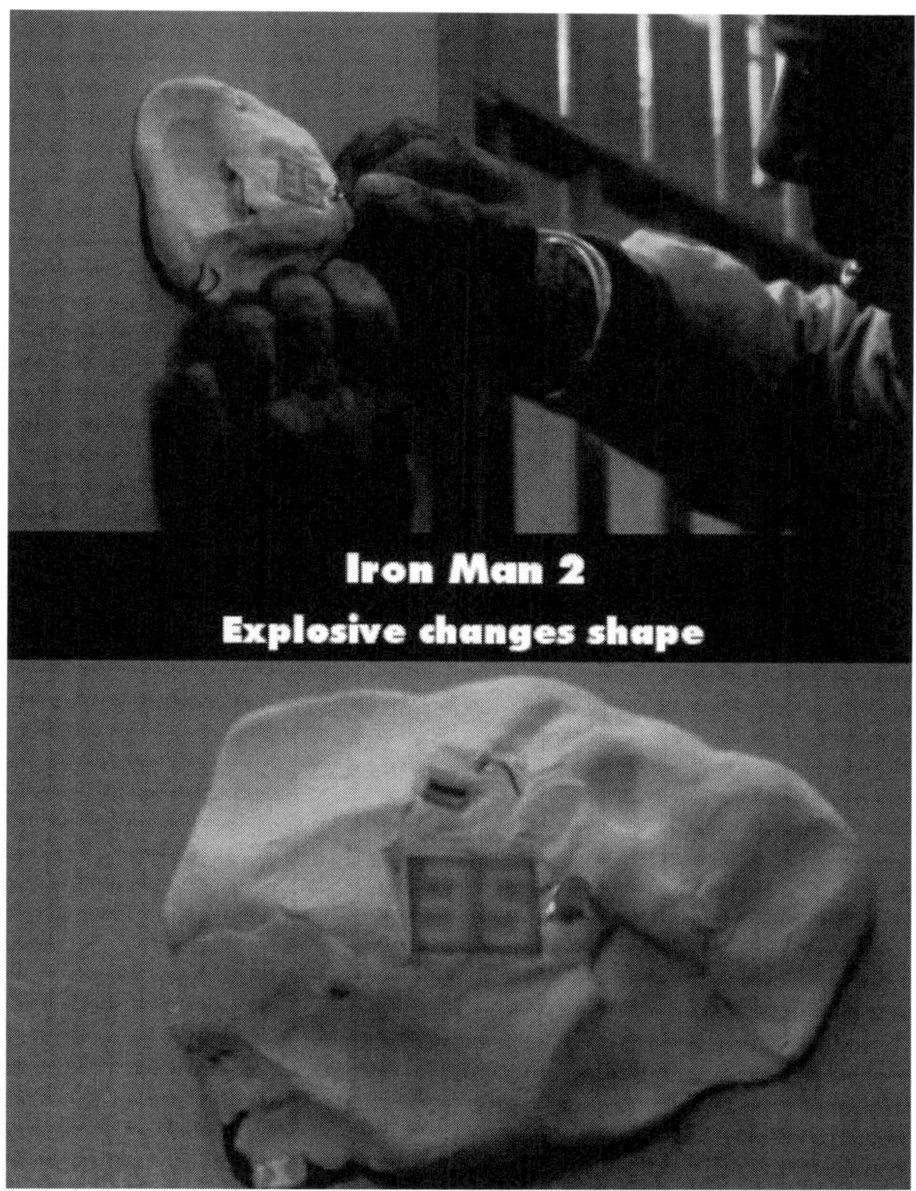

Paramount Studios

In the opening senate scene, the Senator's jug of water keeps turning around and moving closer/away from the nameplate between shots. (00:11:35)

Paramount Studios

During lunch with Ivan, the way Hammer's napkin is tied

around his neck and laid on his shirt keeps changing between shots, despite Hammer not touching it.

When Stark and Rhodey break through the roof of the house the hanging debris from the hole above keeps changing depending on the angle focusing, with hanging parts that appear or disappear randomly.

The scene in the Monaco lounge when Tony Stark and Justin Hammer are sitting down at a table with Christine Everhart to give an interview, Hammer sets his drink on the table while he's standing but then the shot immediately cuts to him sitting down with the drink still in his hand.

When Hammer takes the parrot away from Ivan, the Russian's black jacket keeps swapping from open to closed between angles.

When Ivan crashes Stark's car during the race there is a close-up of Tony's face showing a red scrape on the cornea of his eye. When he puts the suit on there's another close-up of his face inside the armor and both eyes are completely undamaged.

When Natalie and Pepper arrive at the Expo and open the car's door a huge lighting screen gets reflected on the door. (01:32:30)

Paramount Studios

Before Hammer starts eating dessert (and thus much before the "moving spoon and cherry" continuity mistakes), there's a back angle where he dips his spoon into the dessert and starts eating. The angle cuts to a front view with the spoon laying spotless on the saucer, and Hammer saying "I'll start with dessert", and then repeating the whole previous scene as if it were the first time.

In the beginning when Tony's press conference is on TV in Anton Vanko's home, the dialogue exchange between Tony and Christine Everheart has more talking than that same scene in "Iron Man" at the end. In "2", Christine mentions that Tony hates body guards in the exchange, but this is never said in the first "Iron Man".

After the core is removed from Whiplash during the race scene, a stream of blood visibly trails from the corner of his mouth. The shot changes to him spitting and the blood is gone. The shot changes again and it reappears. (00:37:05)

Paramount Studios

IRON MAN 2 TRIVIA

During the film's climax, a young boy in an Iron Man mask is shown standing up to one of the Hammer drones with Iron Man swooping in and destroying the drone and giving the kid the credit. Following Spider-Man's inclusion in the Marvel Cinematic Universe, a fan theory suggested the young boy was Peter Parker, which Marvel Studios President Kevin Feige and Spider-Man actor Tom Holland would later retroactively confirm.

The late DJ Adam Goldstein appears as himself in the movie during Stark's party. The film is dedicated to his memory.

Paramount Studios

Near the end, where Nick Fury and Tony Stark are talking about the Avengers, there is a world map behind them featuring dots. The dots show where the Avengers are: New York (Iron Man); Arctic Circle (Captain America); Europe (Black Widow); Lower Africa (Wakanda for Black Panther); California (Hulk); New Mexico (Thor); Southern Atlantic Ocean (Namor the Sub-Mariner).

During the movie, S.H.I.E.L.D. agent Phil Coulson holds up a circular red, white and blue object with a star and asks where he got it. That was *Captain America's* shield, which also appeared in the first movie in the background, which caused a stir by the fans.

During the fight between Tony and Jim, Tony says "Step up if you think you have what it takes to be a war machine". War Machine is the name of the modified Iron Man armor that Jim wears in the comics.

At the end of the movie when Nick Fury and Tony Stark are talking in the warehouse, the news report seen on the TV is a broadcast from the fight between the Hulk and the army at the university campus from 'The Incredible Hulk' movie.

Attack of the Show host Olivia Munn mentioned she was to have another role in the movie. She played reporter Chess Roberts, but originally had a somewhat bigger role. She was to play a girl at Stark's birthday party who then appears in his bedroom. The scene was eventually cut because it didn't have any comedy in it.

Emily Blunt was originally cast as Black Widow, but scheduling conflicts with Gulliver's Travels caused her to pull out.

The suits were much lighter than the ones used in the first movie, and the legs were left off. From the thighs down the actors were covered in digital markers and the bottom part of the suits were later added with CGI. (As stated in Popular Science, June 2010.)

Spoiler: The film closely resembles several key *Iron Man* stories from the comics. The part when he was drunk references the "Demon in a bottle" storyline, where Rhodey dons an Iron Man suit. The part of him dying is somewhat similar to "Ultimate Iron Man." Also, the idea that his technology is used in a way he doesn't like and having a battle is similar to the "Armor Wars" plot.

Stan Lee makes his customary cameo. He is mistakenly introduced to Tony during the Expo as Larry King.

Paramount Studios

As with the last Iron Man movie, stay till after the end credits for an extra character spot.

Ivan Vanko is a mixture of two *Iron Man* villains: Whiplash, which is the primary part, and Crimson Dynamo. Anton Vanko

(Ivan's father) was the original Dynamo and in the final battle, Vanko wears a suit similar to Dynamo, as it's a hybrid between that and Whiplash.

In the comics, Justin Hammer is an elderly man whose appearance is based on actor Peter Cushing and who is named for the Hammer Horror films in which Cushing appeared.

Fin Fang Foom makes a "cameo" on the street on a billboard.

The boxing training between Happy and Tony references Happy originally being a boxer in the comics.

Ivan has on his fake passport the name Boris Turgenov, the name of Crimson Dynamo in the comics.

The guy who gives the Monaco ticket to Ivan is a member of the ten rings, the alliance ruled by The Mandarin.

A green car at the race has the Roxxon logo, which frequently features in Marvel comics and the MCU.

At the race in Monaco the English pilot is named Chapman - a reference to Joseph Chapman, aka Union Jack in the comics.

THOR MISTAKES

On one of the SHIELD monitors, "perimeter" is spelled "perimiter".

After S.H.I.E.L.D "borrows" Jane's research and Darcy says that they took her iPod, her hair can be seen blowing in the wind in the shots facing her left and not blowing in the shots facing her right.

When the Destroyer arrives amidst the Shield agents, a coffee cup sitting on the dash of one of the vehicles spills over. The next shot it can be seen lying on its side. The reverse angle shot then shows it upright again.(01:21:20)

Paramount Pictures

At the end of the scene where everyone is trying to pull Mjolnir out of the crater, a SHIELD agent is seen pulling up in an SUV at the top of a hill about 50 yards away. When the shot changes to the view from where the SHIELD agent gets out of his SUV and is standing at the top of the hill he is a 1/2 mile away or more.

Paramount Pictures

When Thor and friends first arrive on Frost Giants realm, rocks tumble and create debris - which disappears between shots.

When Thor is walking towards the Destroyer towards the end of the movie, the shadows of the Destroyer, buildings and cars change between shots. Also the Destroyer's height changes from being about 12 feet tall to 8 feet in those shots.

When Jane and Thor are driving out to where the hammer is, we see a lot of side shots showing barbed-wire fence posts passing by on both sides of the truck, but when Jane is distracted and goes a little off the road, we are shown a front shot of her bringing the truck back onto the road, except there are no fence posts or fence anywhere to be seen. Immediately afterwards, we again see side shots with fence posts going by. (00:51:00)

The first time Jane, Darcy and Erik meet Thor, Jane says "Do me a favour and don't be dead. Please. Where did he come from?" But the second time we see them meet him, Darcy suddenly says "Woah, does he need CPR? Because I totally know CPR" right after Jane says "Do me a favour and don't be dead". Extended scene or not, Darcy's line was not there before and it makes no sense for it to be there now because Jane's line is still incomplete when she says it. On top of this, the word "Please" that Jane said earlier is completely gone.

When Thor is trying to recover his hammer from SHIELD, he rolls around on the ground quite a bit and is completely covered in mud. As he is being taken away by the agents at the end of the scene, though, his shirt is clean.

At the end when Loki goes to lock the bifrost on Jotunheim, he's wearing his helmet and carrying Odin's staff. He slides Heimdall's sword into the machinery to open the bifrost and his helmet is gone. He freezes the electrical streams then when Thor comes in to stop him, Loki is wearing his helmet again.

In the desert scene where Jane, Darcy and Eric are getting out of the van to check on the person they just hit, they rush to Thor who is lying on the ground and inside the "bifrost footprint" circle. There are 3 shots following the first wide shot, which focus on Jane, Darcy and Eric, and then back to the wide shot of the 3 surrounding Thor again, but the bifrost print is gone this time. After the Asgard backstory we return to the desert scene and the bifrost print is once again present on the ground.

When Thor tries to get back his hammer, he makes a hole in the fence. Beside that point there are 3 barrels which disappear between shots.

When Dr. Zelvig and Thor are drinking at the bar they get a mug of beer. The bottles of beer in front of them disappear between shots.

When Thor dumps the table with food on it, the bread and cheese change position between shots.

After Thor gets the hammer back and he talks with Coulson and Jane, the sun changes between shots.

The nurse that holds Thor in the clinic has gloves but in the next shots the nurse is a different guy and the gloves are gone.

Before Thor gets the throne of Asgard, there are 2 ice giants looking for the energy cube, but in the next shot there are 3 of them.

THOR TRIVIA

Hang around right until the very end of the credits for a scene which further ties in Thor to a future Avengers movie.

Stan Lee makes his customary appearance as the driver of the white pickup truck that tries to free Mjolnir from the ground.

Paramount Pictures

When Agent Coulson asks for someone to "go up top" to get a good firing position on Thor when he tries to take Mjolnir, it is Clint Barton, AKA Hawkeye, played by Jeremy Renner, who will go on to feature in The Avengers.

Thor enters the pet store and calls for a horse, and then Jane picks him up in her Pinzgauer 716 truck. The joke is that the Pinzgauer is named after an Austrian breed of horse, thus Thor got a ride on a horse.

In the town there is a big picture on a wall that says "Journey into mystery" a nod to the comic book of the same name where Thor was first featured.

In both this film and Marvel Comics, Laufey is Loki's father. In the original Norse mythology, Laufey is Loki's mother.

In Odin's vault lots of artifacts from the comics can be seen such as the eternal flame, tablet of life and time, and briefly the infinity gauntlet of Thanos.

The Orb of Agamotto is seen in the vault of Odin - it's related to Doctor Strange's Eye of Agamotto.

The post credit scene was written and directed by Joss Whedon.

The T-shirt Jane gives Thor has the name tag Donald Blake MD. In the comics Donald Blake is Thor's alter ego.

Odin arrives on Jotunheim riding an eight-legged horse. This horse is called "Sleipnir", and in Norse Mythology is an offspring of Loki.

Before signing on as Odin, Sir Anthony Hopkins had never read a Thor comic, nor even knew anything about the Thor mythology.

CAPTAIN AMERICA: THE FIRST AVENGER MISTAKES

When the action moves to England after the failed award ceremony, the British Union Flag hanging from the wall is upside down. The broad white band should be at the top left (nearest the top of the flagpole).

In the scenes set outside the Hydra bases, the tracked armoured personnel carriers seen are FV432s. These vehicles entered service with the British army in the 1960s, and thus were never even seen during WW2 when the film is set.

After Steve throws Heinz Kruger, the assassin sent to kill him, out of his boat, both Steve and Heinz are bone dry despite being fully submerged in water only moments before.

During the chase scene involving Rogers and the Hydra spy that happened after Rogers got his new powers, the windshield of the cab the agent was driving was shot twice. In some shots, especially once Rogers landed on the roof of the cab, the windshield has no holes.

In the scene where they break into the train from its roof, you can notice that despite the high speed and the consistent wind, Captain America's fellows have no difficulties in running, standing up still, and even jumping, like they felt no air resistance.

Moreover, you can see that their hair is not moving at all, completely missing to realize any "windy" effect.

In the closing credits, during the montage of World War II posters, the American flag appears wrapped around a cannon barrel. The flag has 50 stars, not the then-correct 48.

When Captain America is ready to jump out the plane, he is looking at Peggy Carter when he reaches for his goggles, the angle changes to the outside and Cap is seen with one hand out the plane and the other in, with his goggles up. it switches back inside and his goggles are on.

Oddly for a movie set in the 1940's when nearly half the U.S. population smoked, absolutely no one in the movie is seen smoking. More recognizable in the bar scenes, almost everyone in that bar would have been smoking.

The windscreen on the flying wing appears to be completely intact when it is discovered in the present. Not only is it implausible to believe it survived a head-on crash without being damaged, but also during the final fight on board, it receives several bullet holes.

The German Stielgranaten - as well as other traditional German WW II hand grenades - did not have a ring and pin like the ones the Allies used, but had a string which had to be pulled hard in order to arm them. Thus they wouldn't make such a distinct 'ping' as they do in the movie.

At one point the Colonel references "MI-6" which is the current British term for their intelligence service. However this terminology didn't exist until after the war. During WWII it would have been referred to as Special Operations Executive or SOE.

In the section during the movie reel, there is footage of the 1939 world's fair in New York. The Unisphere is shown. Unfortunately, the Unisphere was constructed in 1964 for the 1964-1965 world's fair. The Perisphere (and Trylon) were the centerpiece of the 1939 fair. The Perisphere was a sphere 200 feet in diameter. The Unisphere is still standing in flushing meadows park in New York city.

At the end of the chase through New York, when Steve picks up the taxicab door and uses it as a shield, he has a wet spot or stain on his right knee. Moments later it is gone.

During the final battle on board the 'flying wing' between Captain America and Red Skull, the finish on CA's shield appears damaged and scorched. Yet in the opening sequence of the movie when his shield is discovered under ice inside the frozen 'flying wing' it appears undamaged.

In one scene, Steve Rogers is shown wearing a Combat Infantry Badge (CIB) on his pocket flap, below his ribbons, with his jump wings above the ribbons. Proper wearing would be CIB on top, jump wings, then the ribbons, all above the pocket flap.

When Rogers and Agent Carter are about to enter the antique shop for the first time, one shot shows Rogers raising both arms to place his cap on his head. The shot changes and Rogers' hands are now down, and he begins to raise them again.

The early scene in the movie theatre is in 1943. In the opening newsreel a Sherman Firefly tank is shown. This tank was not made until early 1944 [the long barrel and spherical muzzle brake are distinctive]. Even if we were to assume the tank was made earlier in the Marvel Cinematic Universe due to people like Stark working for the Allies it still would not be shown in a newsreel anyway for security reasons, with German spies and sympathizers present in the US during the war. (00:09:30)

Dr. Erskine says he lives in Queens at 73rd Street and Utopia Parkway. Actually, 73rd Street is well to the west of Utopia Parkway (both run north-south). Erskine must have meant 73rd Avenue, which does cross Utopia Parkway.

When Schmidt sets the self-destruct timer at the Hydra base, the clocks countdown at twice the speed of real-time.

Colonel Phillips walks into the cell that holds Dr. Zola, while carrying a dinner tray. When he puts it on the table the salt and pepper shakers and the glass of milk are on Colonel Phillips' side of the table. In the next shot you can see Colonel Phillips turning the tray around to Dr. Zola. After he refuses the food and Colonel Philips makes a snappy remark about cyanide, Colonel Philips turns the tray back, so the shakers are on his side. But then when he starts eating they are on Dr. Zola's side again. He does move the glass of milk with his right hand and grabs the knife and fork with his left, making it impossible for him to have moved the shakers. (01:26:00 - 01:26:40)

CAPTAIN AMERICA: THE FIRST AVENGER TRIVIA

Some of the members of Captain America's wartime elite squad are taken from Marvel Comics WWII based "Sgt Nick Fury and the Howling Commandos" - such as Dum Dum Duggan and Gabe Jones.

Before Steve Rogers exits the chamber that changes him into Captain America, the sound effect for the machine winding down is the same one as for the rocket pack shutting down in The Rocketeer, another Joe Johnston movie.

Throughout the whole movie, all of the laser guns have the exact same sound effect as the gun Iron Man shoots out of his hands.

When Steve Rogers is performing at a USO show, he play punches a guy portraying Adolf Hitler in the face. The cover for the very first Captain America comic had Captain America actually punching Hitler in the face.

At the World Expo there is a display with a mannequin in a red suit inside a glass tube, a reference to the original Human Torch Jim Hammond who fought alongside Captain America in the comics.

Stan Lee cameo: When Captain America did not come out for

one of his shows, a short man came out to tell the announcer he would not be appearing. Stan Lee says "I thought he would be taller."

Paramount Pictures

When Captain America is approaching Red Skull's lair in the Alps, one of the German sentries lets out a Wilhelm scream when he gets knocked off his motorcycle.

When we first see the German scientist Arnim Zola, we only see his face appearing distorted through a yellowish lens. This is a nod to his comic book counterpart - in the comics, Zola exists within a robotic body, with his face appearing on a monitor on the robot's chest.

There is a post credit scene and a brief advance of the Avengers film.

Laura Haddock plays a dancer that asks Steve for an autograph. She later played the mother of Star Lord in Guardians of the

Galaxy.

When Arnim Zola is gathering his papers,after Captain America goes on the rescue mission in the factory,we see a blueprint for Zola's robotic body.A nod to the comics and possibly foreshadowing the events of Captain America:The Winter Soldier.

Bucky takes the shield of Cap for a brief moment as reference to the comics where he has taken the mantle of Captain America.

At the expo Stark shows a flying red car that's the same colour as the Iron Man armour.

THE AVENGERS MISTAKES

A reflector screen is visible on Hawkeye's sunglasses at the very end when Thor and a restrained Loki are returning, presumably, to Asgard. (02:06:10)

In the scene in Stuttgart, we see a "reserved parking" sign written as "Reservierten Parken". First of all, this is grammatically wrong - if used at all, it should be "Reserviertes Parken". But you wouldn't find a sign in Germany saying that. They say "Reservierter Parkplatz".

Throughout the film, Tony Stark's chest ring can be seen glowing through his shirt except for two occasions when it's suddenly off - after Loki escapes from the helicarrier, and when Loki and Tony Stark are talking in Stark tower, even when he's wearing the same shirt. (01:35:30)

Walt Disney Pictures

You can see the blue screens on Bruce Banner's glasses when Tony Stark is talking to him about embracing the Hulk rather than disliking it. (00:57:40)

In Stuttgart, the German police cars use the wrong lights (they should be blue instead of orange-yellow) and license plate marking arrangements. (00:39:40)

When Hawkeye is breaking onto the Helicarrier, he and some snipers break down a duct cover and enter. When the cover lands on the floor, it is resting away from some pipes with some slats missing. As soon as Hawkeye enters the duct, the cover is now resting against the pipes, and the slats have reappeared. (01:10:35)

Walt Disney Pictures

When Thor lands beside the overturned car on the Park Ave viaduct in front of Grand Central, the car has a dent between its fender and tire, but in the next closeup that dent has vanished. (02:04:10)

Walt Disney Pictures

When one of the computer operators resumed playing Galaga, the sound effect heard is for an enemy ship attempting to capture the player's ship, but what's shown on screen is normal gameplay.

When Iron Man and Thor are fighting, Thor grabs Iron Man's wrist at one point. In the next shot, he is holding him by the forearm. (00:46:55)

When Tony goes after the nuke, there is a huge cut visible above his right eyebrow (or viewer's left). Later on after his face mask is removed, his right eyebrow is completely visible in the shot, even with the helmet in the way, and the cut is nowhere in sight. (02:00:00 - 02:03:00)

Walt Disney Pictures

During the big battle against the Chitauri, Captain America is zapped with a blaster bolt. When Thor helps him to his feet we can see a significant amount of damage done to his suit, just below the star on the right hand side. But later on after Iron Man destroys the Chitauri ship with the nuke, the damage is completely gone. (01:59:25 - 02:02:40)

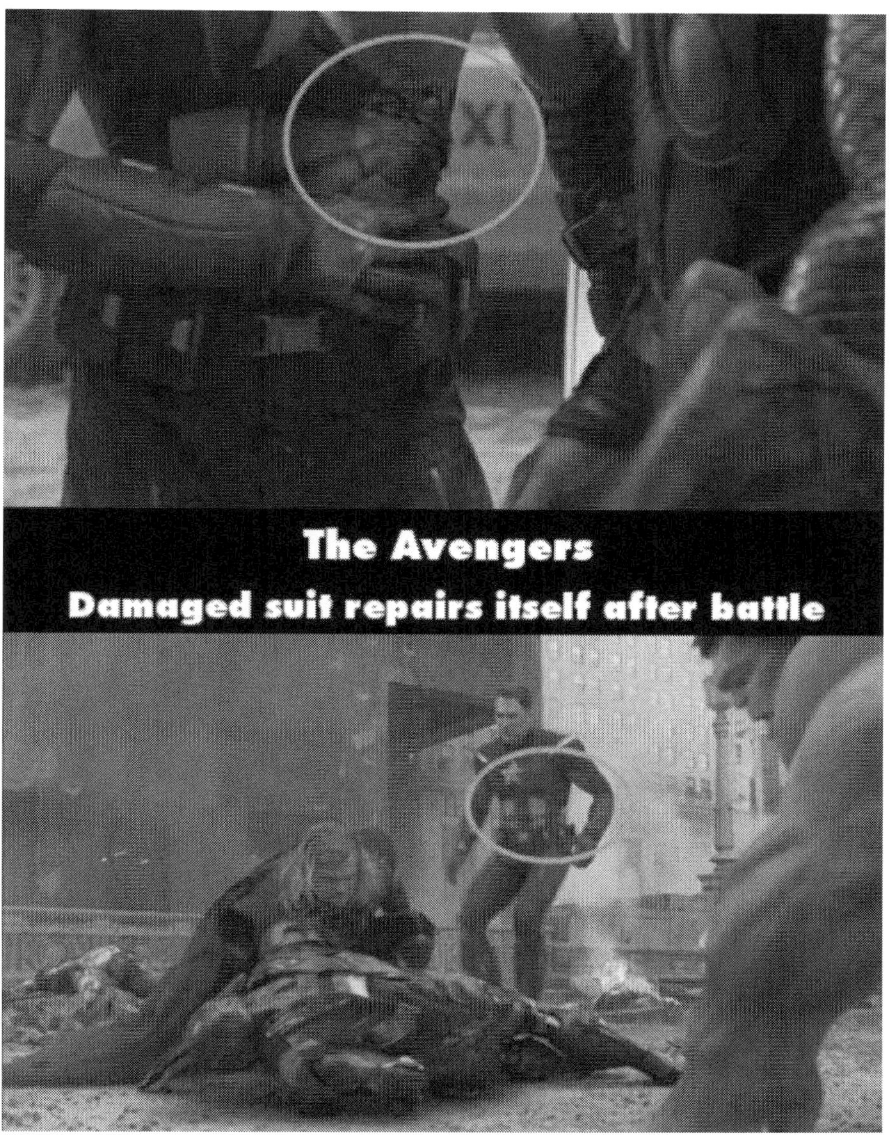

Walt Disney Pictures

The Mark 7 takes 9 seconds to assemble - give or take. Judging by the view of the Chrysler Building, Stark Tower is about 300 meters high. Even if you discount the time it takes for the suit to catch up with Tony, 9 seconds is too long, he would hit the ground before the suit would fully assemble. (01:41:35)

When Steve Rogers first meets Bruce Banner, Rogers' hair keeps changing between being neat and being blown apart, depending on the angle. (00:32:35)

The video game company NAMCO Bandai is misspelled twice as "NAMECO Bandai" in the end credits, although fixed in the home video version.

When the plane lands on the aircraft carrier, it is about to land on a yellow mark on the ground. The angle cuts and it's now landing in front of it. Then from the aerial angle it lands in the middle of both lanes, but a frame later it's on the right lane. Finally, the landing signal officer swaps from standing in front of the plane waving his arms, to several meters behind standing still. (00:31:45)

During the battle of New York, Thor has just landed next to an upturned silver car. The rubble around the car changes/ moves. The most noticeable is one wedged next to the front right wheel. The piece becomes much bigger in the next shot. (01:50:25)

Walt Disney Pictures

When Steve and Coulson land on the Helicarrier, you can see two wings on the edge of the Quinjet they were in and they are both closed up. Next shot, as Romanoff approaches the Quinjet and Steve and Coulson exit, we can see one of the wings is completely open. (00:30:35)

In the scene where Natasha Romanoff does a flip while tied to the chair, you can see her stunt double at the very end of her flip. Her arms become much more muscular. (00:14:30)

The Königsstraße in Stuttgart is located in the city's main shopping area, not its cultural center as the film would suggest. (00:37:20)

When Maria Hill is being attended to after she gets hurt, her earpiece is on the left side of her face. In the next shot she is talking to Nick Fury and her earpiece is on the right.

THE AVENGERS TRIVIA

While on the helicarrier, Tony Stark is wearing a Black Sabbath T-shirt, the band who released the song "Iron Man".

Mark Ruffalo is the only actor to be credited as both Bruce Banner and the Hulk.

When Bruce Banner is explaining to everyone how he can't die, he tells them that he once put a gun in his mouth and pulled the trigger, but that the Hulk spit out the bullet. This was supposed to be the original opening scene for The Incredible Hulk starring Edward Norton.

Robert Downey Jr. jokingly improvised the line referring to one of the techie's playing Galaga. Director Joss Whedon loved the line so much, he added in the later shot where we see the techie literally playing Galaga.

In the final scene of the film, as Tony is unfolding the blueprints for the new Stark Tower, if you look very carefully (slo-mo may be necessary) you can see files with a symbol representing each Avenger in the upper right corner of each file - Captain America's shield, Thor's hammer, etc. The implication being that Tony will build a section of Stark Tower for each of his friends.

During the scene where Thor and Loki are talking near the cliff, two ravens are seen flying overhead. In Norse mythology Odin has two ravens named Huginn and Muninn who give Odin information from Midgard (Earth).

Stay during the credits, there's an extra bonus scene after the animated credits and before the main (scrolling) credits. Those of you dedicated Marvel fans will have to explain what is in the scene to everyone else. There is also a second bonus scene at the very end of the credits.

Thor's three main costumes are referenced in this film. His sleeveless first appearance, armored second, and capeless ultimate looks are all seen.

For the post-credit scene where the group are eating shawarma together, Chris Evans had to wear a prosthetic jaw, because he had grown a beard for another movie and couldn't shave it off. It's also why he's resting his head on his hand through the entire scene, conveniently covering up most of his face.

Stan Lee had two cameos in the movie but his first appearance was cut. In the scene when Steve Rogers is at the cafe seen in the final fight where he first encounters the waitress who had become infatuated with Captain America after he saves her. Stan Lee basically calls Steve a moron for not asking for her phone number.

Paul Bettany, who voices Jarvis in this and the standalone Iron Man films, hasn't seen any of them. In an interview he said "This is robbery. I walk in, I say some lines on a piece of paper for two hours, and then they give me a bag of money and I leave and I go about my day...I've never seen one of them...It's not because of any snobbishness, it's just not my thing."

From a bird's-eye view, the layout of the helicarrier's bridge forms the SHIELD Eagle logo.

After the Hulk falls into the isolated building and wakes up as Bruce Banner, the security guard who assists him and subsequently asks: "Are you an alien?", is Harry Dean Stanton from the classic film 'Alien'.

The Avengers co-creator Stan Lee makes his usual cameo. This time as a man being interviewed by a news reporter asking about superheroes, at the end of the movie.

Walt Disney Pictures

When Stan Lee is being interviewed, in the top left corner of the screen Stan Lee is one it says "FILE: A113" A-113 references a graphic design and character animation classroom at California Institute of the Arts, and is often referenced by alumni.

There is a small screen showing the heat signature in the room where Loki is being held which shows that he has a cold body temperature because he is a frost giant.

Walt Disney Pictures

When Thor and Hulk battle on the helicarrier, Thor hits Hulk, who collides with a Harrier jump jet. The prop Harrier which Hulk hits is the very same one that Arnold Schwarzenegger flew in True Lies.

At the Shield headquarters there is a plate referring to project Pegasus. In the comics that was created to research alternative forms of energy, and as a prison for super powered persons.

The photo of Cap in Tony's tower has the number #25 - the issue number of the comics in which Captain America dies.

The Russian general who speaks with Natasha is Giorgi Leuco, who in the comics is an enemy of Iron Man.

IRON MAN 3
MISTAKES

When the Iron Patriot armor is shot at on Air Force One, the bullets ricochet and smash a window. The windows on Air Force One are bulletproof. (01:32:55)

After Tony gets the armor back at the Mandarin's hideout and meets up with Rhodes, they go by boat to the harbor. On the way Tony calls the Vice President - during this scene the VP's phone changes, note the camera on the back of the phone is visible, but in another shot right after, it is a completely flat back panel.(01:30:10)

When Harley asks Tony what the light is coming from his chest, Tony responds "an electromagnet." Harley replies "What does it power?" An electromagnet is not a source of power. The arc reactor is the power source which powers both the electromagnet (to keep Tony safe from the shrapnel near his heart) and the Iron Man suit. (00:43:25)

When Tony is sending a holiday greeting to The Mandarin, he has sunglasses on. Then in the shot from behind, he doesn't have any glasses on. Then they reappear in the next shot and then he takes off the sunglasses. (00:28:55)

When Tony is in his garage injecting his arm, his chest piece is glowing brightly through his shirt, however, the very next shot when he is wiping his arm with the alcohol pad, his chest piece is suddenly turned off.(00:05:15)

Walt Disney Pictures

When Tony is giving his address to the Mandarin through the media the reporter in front of him has a cell phone which changes design between shots. (00:28:50)

Before Tony sends a holiday greeting to the Mandarin his car is pointed one way when he gets in, then the car faces the other direction. (00:28:45 - 00:29:45)

When Ellen Brandt is confronting the Police Chief of Rose Hill, TN at the bar. The weapon that is visible that Brandt takes is a semi-automatic with a single stack magazine. The weapon which she shoots has a double stack magazine. (00:54:10)

When Maya is trying to get Killian to let Tony go, she holds a dose of Extremis to her neck and says "1200 cc's - A dose half this size, I'm dead." 1200 cc's is 1.2 litres, or over 40 oz/2 pints. What she's holding is barely the size of a cell phone, nowhere near that volume. (01:22:50)

When Tony and Rhodes leave the Mandarin's mansion, Tony has blood on his left eye and cheek, which changes to the other eye between shots, then changes again at the boat. (01:30:25)

Tony is in the bedroom with Maya Hansen, Happy is seen closing the sliding door. With the door just inches from being fully closed, a quick cut to Tony and Maya kissing, then back to Happy, and the door is almost fully open, with Happy in the process of closing it again just as the plant explodes. (00:03:45)

How come the Extremis serum was able to regenerate Ellen Brandt's arm but not repair the scar on her face? According to the movie, the serum is supposed to rewrite the body's genetic code and constantly repair damaged cells, so her face should have been restored to its original state, just like her missing arm. Even if she had been born with the scar the serum would have healed it, just like it healed all of Aldrich Killian's physical impairments. (00:51:40)

When Jarvis wakes Tony up when he is in Tennessee, there is quite a lot of blood on his face. But when he takes off his mask, so before he had any time to wipe it off, the amount of blood decreases significantly.(00:39:50 - 00:40:30)

When Stark gets trapped by the water tank he is completely

soaked. When he walks back to the car with the boy he is completely dry and his hair is restyled with not enough time for this to happen. (00:56:50 - 00:57:55)

When Tony Stark and Col. Rhodes confront the Mandarin in his chair the hammer for the Beretta is forward after Rhodes loaded a new magazine. The hammer is shown in the back position in a subsequent shot. It happens twice during this scene. (01:30:05)

When Tony is creating his weapons, one shot shows the electric glove he is wearing to be designed for his left hand. Later on, when he is in the Mandarin's mansion, he attacks one of the guards with the electric glove, only now the glove is on his right hand. (01:12:50 - 01:14:10)

At the end Tony drives an Audi R-8 e-tron, which is an electric car, and while it has a sound system to produce an artificial engine noise, it doesn't sound like what is heard. (01:59:20)

When Tony's house is destroyed by the Mandarin, watch closely when Pepper is blown through the air, just before Tony attaches his suit to her - she's very obviously wearing high-heeled shoes that would make it impossible for her feet/ankles to fit correctly into the suit without them being crunched up by the suit's boots. But later on, when she gets out, if you listen, you can hear the "clicking" of her unbroken heels as she runs around.

In the scene in Tennessee, when Tony is being chased by the glowing "homeland security" lady. He throws a jug of oil and lights it on fire with the red hot handcuffs that he takes off. Then he somehow manages to slip a set of dog tags in a microwave and turns it on. This is to create a spark to explode the gas line that he pulls from the wall, which somehow isn't ignited by the large grease fire in the same room. (00:57:55)

When the Mark 42 is "done" assembling for the first time, in Tony's workshop, a digital model of the suit appears in the lower right corner of the screen. In this render, the suit is complete, but a moment later there is still one piece missing, which hits Tony so hard the entire suit falls apart. (00:07:30)

IRON MAN 3 TRIVIA

Once again, Stan Lee makes his usual cameo. This time, he appears as a judge at the Christmas pageant.

Walt Disney Pictures

The extremis soldier that blows up at the theatre is named Jack Taggart, who in the comics was another armored villain, known as Firepower.

Stay till to the end of the credits once again for an extra scene. This time featuring an unexpected cameo and after that a tag line appears that says,"Tony Stark Will Return".

The mandarin has a version of Captain America's shield tattoo on the back of his neck, with an Anarchy symbol instead of the star.

Ellen Brandt in the comics is an agent of AIM, who was a lover of Ted Sallis. Dr. Sallis tried to make the super soldier serum and later became the Man-Thing.

While Stark is watching Happy's hologram clue, there is an image of a dragon that's a reference to Fin Fang Foom, an alien dragon who appeared in strange tales #89 in 1961.

When Pepper gets home for the first time and is looking at the letters/drawings from the kids, one is from "Mitch B." Mitch Bell is an associate producer of IM3.

Warren Ellis, the writer of the comic book series named Extremis, which this film takes cues from, is referenced by the President.

Professor Yensin appears in tales of suspense #39 in 1963, and helped Tony to make the first suit in Iron Man 1.

When Killian shows Pepper the universe by mistake, that footage is the same as seen in Captain America: The First Avenger.

Bruce Banner makes a cameo in a post credit scene.

One of the guys who is watching Tony before the Mark 42 flies to him is the same actor that replaces Whiplash in the French jail in Iron Man 2.

Slattery's speedboat, a gift from Killian, is named 'Cordelia', after the favourite daughter of King Lear. Killian told Stark that Slattery had played Lear in Croydon.

The dragon tattoo on Killian's chest is a reference to Fin Fang Foom, an alien dragon that appeared in astonishing tales #23 and #24 from 1974.

The Sun Oracle server used by Tony is in the comics owned by Namor, another Avenger.

THOR: THE DARK WORLD MISTAKES

In the final fight scene with Malekith, Thor falls through a portal that brings him to Charing Cross station, where the lady on the train tells him he has to ride 3 stops to get to Greenwich. Charing Cross is not on the Jubilee Line and so not directly connected to Greenwich - even then it's a lot more than 3 stops. (01:33:45)

In the scene where Thor tells Jane to hold on, she's on Thor's right side and Mjölnir (the hammer) is in his left hand. As they are traveling through the Bifröst to Asgard, the position of each has changed. (00:28:20)

Walt Disney Pictures

When the aether enters Jane, just before she ends up back on earth, she is cross-like in a sea of red, but she is wearing a breast-plate. She does not get given this until she is taken to Asgard 15 minutes later.

Sif has a wound on the left side of her forehead which disappears when she arrives at Asgard.

In Asgard, right after Frigga has been captured, a Kursed Algrim is holding her by the shoulder. In the next shot he is holding her around the neck.

When Loki is nearly sucked into the vortex, his hands are empty. However, in the first shot after Thor rescues him when they fall to the ground, he suddenly has his dagger in his left hand.

When Kursed Algrim stabs Frigga, the sword goes in but doesn't come out.

At the end, Jane and the others are sitting at the table eating. Right when Jane says "we committed treason as we left" she is holding her spoon. The shot changes and now the spoon is in the bowl and she picks it up.

Thor has a massive boulder thrown at him. He ends up with a cut on his right forehead that moves to his left in another scene and back to his right in the next. Along with inconsistencies to the scar and placement at the end when he's holding Loki. (01:18:50 - 01:20:20)

The wounds on Thor's forehead change from fresh to dry then fresh back again, and even become larger in the last fight.

When Thor, Loki and Jane make their escape from Asgard, Jane is lying on her left side. The following cut, she is on her right side.

Lady Sif's shield is pierced by an arrow during the opening battle. In all subsequent shots, the hole vanishes and the shield is intact.

As Thor and Odin watch the people practicing battling, Odin says Thor has earned his gratitude. Thor says "Thank you" lowering his head. In the next shot, his head is suddenly raised. (00:10:35)

After the battle of Vanaheim has ended, the scene cuts to Asgard where Odin watches people practicing battling and is joined by Thor. The shot after Odin says "Vanaheim secure?" shows Thor with his head half turned to Odin. Next shot he's suddenly looking at the battling people without his head turned an inch. (00:10:15)

THOR: THE DARK WORLD TRIVIA

Stan Lee makes his usual cameo, this time as a patient at the asylum where Selvig is being held.

Walt Disney Pictures

The kiss between Thor and Jane after the credits doesn't actually feature Natalie Portman - due to scheduling issues she wasn't available, so Chris Hemsworth's wife Elsa Pataky put on a wig and filmed the scene.

In the film a raven lands on Odin's arm. In Norse Mythology Odin has two ravens that fly through the realms and deliver information to him, they are called Huginn and Muninn.

Stay during the credits for a scene part way through and another one at the end.

Thor takes the head of a statue of Bor as a reference to the comics, where Bor is killed by Thor.

According to Norse mythology, Loki was to be eternally bound far below Asgard by Odin, as punishment for betraying/killing Odin's other beloved son Balder. Loki's eternal imprisonment for betraying Thor reflects this tale.

Adam's Warlock's cocoon can be seen in the collector's place.

Thor appears to lose his hand. Someone's lost a limb in nearly every MCU film since Iron Man 3.

CAPTAIN AMERICA: THE WINTER SOLDIER MISTAKES

When Cap is driving the blue Chevrolet Silverado with Black Widow, the gear shift is in the up locked position, not lower on the column, indicating the truck was towed in the scene. (00:54:45)

During the Nick Fury chase scene that takes place in D.C., several black and white state highway 6 signs are visible. These signs are unique to Ohio. Route 6 goes straight through downtown Cleveland where the scene was filmed. Plus during other chase scenes several Cleveland landmarks are visible in the background.(00:28:30)

After the SHIELD agents have rescued the hostages, Steve begins a fight with one of the terrorists who tells him to take off his helmet. Steve takes it off and drops it beside him, leaving it on the floor. After Steve kicks the terrorist and runs over to him, you'll see in the next shot that the helmet is still right beside him, despite his run. (00:11:35)

When Captain America takes on the plane outside, the concourse behind him gets shot up and he destroys the plane, which crashes. A little while later the strike team leave the base in convoy along the same concourse that got shot up - there's no damage, and no crashed plane.

Nick Fury's black SUV gets hit by several police cars - the driver's airbag deploys and is visible in all shots until the SUV eventually escapes, at which point the airbag has disappeared.

When Steve is at the Smithsonian, he reads the biography of his friend Bucky. At the start of the description, the bio reads "Born in 1916...", but at the bottom of the description, it reads "Bucky Barnes: 1917 - 1944."(00:18:35)

When Steve leaps from the helicopter and onto the boat, he lands in the water. As soon as he gets on board the boat, he is completely dry. (00:05:00)

When Steve and Romanoff "switch on" Arnim Zola, Zola says "I may not be the man I was when the Captain took me prisoner in 1945." In the first Captain America, it was shown Steve took Zola into custody the same day as his friend Bucky supposedly died. However, the bio of Bucky shown at the Smithsonian earlier in the film said that he died in 1944. (01:00:25)

The location in DC has latitude and longitude both as N/S - longitude is an east/west factor. (00:13:05)

Walt Disney Pictures

After the Winter Soldier blows up the car he assumed Romanoff was hiding behind, she sneaks up behind him and kicks the gun out of his hand. When he throws her at one of the cars, the gun is on the road to the left of some yellow lines, next to a car. A few shots later, when the Winter Soldier picks up the gun, the gun and car have both moved - the gun is now right on the lines, the car is still the same distance from it.(01:18:00)

Walt Disney Pictures

When Nick lights his lighter to burn all of his stuff, two white screens are visible in his glasses. (01:59:00)

When Steve and Romanoff are lying against the knocked over

blinds after dodging the grenade, there is a box shown with some papers in it between them. The first shot shows a white piece of paper sticking furthest out of the box. Next shot, the furthest piece of paper sticking out of the box is now a peach coloured piece of paper. (00:12:45)

In the scene where Nick Fury is showing Steve the new Helicarriers, just as Nick says "The satellites can read a terrorist's DNA before he steps outside the spider hole", the two are shown turning around. Nick is shown turning around almost completely and Steve is shown only turning half way. In the next shot, Nick is suddenly turned only half way, facing Steve. (00:16:20)

On the bridge when the Winter Soldier attacks; when Steve, Natasha, and Sam are in the car stopped, a Hummer rear ends them and starts to push the car. The first shot of the Winter Soldier shows various cars near him. Then a brief shot of Sam, and back to the Winter Soldier and the various cars have changed drastically.

When Zola's algorithm is deployed and begins acquiring targets, we see a "grid" with the targets chosen. On the right, just above the pictures of the targets, there is a line indicating "targets acquired." Then we see the guns and then a counter indicating the amount of targets acquired, from 210,000 and up, but the next grid we see, in the "targets acquired" line says 133,213 and up. Besides, all the grids have the same pictures, but in different order.

As Captain America and the S.H.I.E.L.D team head to the Lemurian Star in the Indian Ocean, both coordinates are North. Longitude has to be E/W and the coordinates link to the Arabian Sea, to the north of the Indian Ocean. (00:03:30)

Walt Disney Pictures

When confronting Nick Fury about Black Widow's mission aboard the Lemurian Star, Cap puts his hands on his hips. In the next shot, his hands are down at his sides. The two shots alternate several times, showing the error. (00:14:20)

When Rogers is launched through the front window of the bus after the Winter Soldier shoots him with a grenade, the bus is hit by a truck and flips. But if you look closely, the damage is minimal. On the truck it would qualify as a fender bender, and the dent in the bus looks like it was made with one decent swing from a sledgehammer. No way was that collision powerful enough to flip a fourteen ton bus on its side. (01:14:50)

There is a sweat stain on Sam's jumper after he finishes jogging with Steve. As he lies against a tree, the stain is around the neck area and some of it is partway down his jumper. When Steve helps him up, the stain has reduced to just sweat around his neck. (00:01:40)

At one point near the beginning of the infiltration of the helicarriers, Captain America's chinstrap has a twist from his right jaw down to where it covers his chin. This is visible in two shots.

The next time his right side is shown afterward, the twist is gone. The chinstrap is too tight for it to have flipped on its own accidentally, and the pad which covers his chin is molded so it wouldn't have sat properly on his face even if it had somehow flipped around. There were undoubtedly several prop helmets made, and this one must have been put together incorrectly.

CAPTAIN AMERICA: THE WINTER SOLDIER TRIVIA

SPOILER: At the end on Nick Fury's gravestone, under his name is the passage from Ezekiel 25:17: "The path of the righteous man is beset..." This was the start of a big monologue made famous by Samuel L Jackson in Pulp Fiction.

Spoiler: Brock Rumlow at the end of the film is in the hospital, badly burned. In the comics, this is how he becomes the villain Crossbones. He later appears as that character in Avengers: Age of Ultron.

When the helicarriers start their targeting for people and locations to destroy, for a brief moment you can see "Anthony Stark" shown in the fully repaired Stark Tower, now the Avengers Tower (it has the big Avengers A logo now).

Stan Lee makes his customary cameo appearance as a security guard at the Smithsonian who is present when Steve Rogers steals his original Captain America suit from the museum display.

Walt Disney Pictures

The film producers actually put a lot of thought into Steve's notebook of things to catch up on. The producers thought it would have been a good idea to show Steve's notebook as a way to see that Steve Rogers is a man out of time. Since the idea is that Captain America can feel like he's a hero, not just for America, but the whole world, the producers set up an internet campaign from each different territory to weigh in on the different things Steve would have in his notebook. The campaign would work as the people would have to vote on 20 things Steve could have missed in the last 70 years. The top 5 vote getters from each country ended up getting implemented into each region's version of the film. The bottom 5 options (Thai food, Star Wars/ Trek, Nirvana (band), Rocky (Rocky II?) and the Troubleman soundtrack) remained in each version of the film.

When Cap and Black Widow are driving to his old army base in New Jersey, she asks him where he learned how to steal a car. This is a reference to the 1990 Captain America film, in which

Captain America steals someone's car on two separate occasions.

Director Joe Russo appears in the film as Dr. Fine, one of the S.H.I.E.L.D. doctors who operates on Nick Fury. In the credit, Russo uses the alias Gozie Agbo.

There are two additional scenes in the credits. One part-way through connected to The Avengers: Age of Ultron, and a second shorter scene right at the very end.

At the hijacked ship, Captain America fights the enemy leader, Batroc, who is loosely based on the comic villain, Batroc the Leaper. The movie Batroc shares the same colour scheme, is also French, but unlike the cartoon version, does mixed martial arts (with a little jumping).

Natasha has a small arrow on her necklace as a reference to Hawkeye.

When Jasper Sitwell was being interrogated by Captain America, The Falcon and Black Widow, he mentions a couple of people Hydra is targeting. One in particular is a certain neurosurgeon named Stephen Strange. Otherwise known as Sorcerer Supreme, Doctor Strange, a future member of The Avengers who will have his own film in Phase 3 of the MCU.

Danny Pudi has a small cameo as the techie who lets Captain America into the communications room near the end of the film. Pudi is one of the stars of the cult TV-series "Community." Directors Joe and Anthony Russo, in addition to directing this film, also directed a number of episodes of "Community."

Romanoff mentions Operation Paperclip at one point, calling it a Shield operation. In reality, it was a large operation conducted by the American government, in which hundreds of Nazi scientists were recruited. One of the most famous subjects was Werner Von Braun, who designed the V2, but went on to make the Saturn V rocket for the Apollo program.

GUARDIANS OF THE GALAXY MISTAKES

When the Dark Aster enters the atmosphere at the end of the film, its wings untwist as it descends, in most of the scenes afterwards and the hologram the ship's wings are still twisted, then later during the battle they untwist again.

At the end of the movie, when Star Lord is dancing to distract Ronan, Ronan is holding the hammer so the head is to his left, but when Drax shoots the hammer the head is now on his right. It changes instantly between shots. (01:41:45)

Rocket is canonically four feet tall and weighs fifty-five pounds, about the size of a six-year-old. At the end of the movie, when carrying a knocked-out Rocket, Quill's arms are not tense as if he was holding that much weight.

When Quill and Gamora first meet and get into a fight, Gamora grabs the Orb Quill is carrying and runs. Quill throws a sort of laser-based "lasso device" that snares her legs and causes her to fall. She pulls it off, and immediately in the next shot, it's vanished from the ground between cuts. It also had mechanical components, so even if the laser vanished, the mechanical pieces should still be on the ground.

Walt Disney Pictures

The space between Drax and Ronan changes between shots when Drax tries to stab him.

During the prison break, Gamora kicks a guard with a black baton that she needs to take. When she first kicks him, her hands are up, and the next shot she's grabbing his wrist and the baton is in front of her body. In the next shot, it's behind her head and the next shot the baton has moved to a 3rd position, across her leg.

At the end when the ship crashes that part of the city is leveled - we see injured people, but no one is covered in dust or dirt thrown up by the impact - everyone is clean.

After Ronan pushes Rocket away near the end of the film, Peter is seen with his hand near his face. However, in the very next shot, his hands are by his sides.

GUARDIANS OF THE GALAXY TRIVIA

Stan Lee makes his customary appearance when Rocket Raccoon is sweeping the plaza for likely targets - he is seen chatting up a young lady.

Walt Disney Pictures

The planet the orb is found on is called Morag. In the comics Morag is the first leader of the Kree, whose actions started the eon long Kree/Skrull war.

When the main characters are doing the slow motion "hero strut" just before the battle to save Nova Prime (the song 'Cherry Bomb' is playing), watch Gamora... She lets out a huge yawn.

At the beginning Star Lord finds a horse-like skeleton, most probably a brief reference to Beta Ray Bill - one of the few other characters that can hold Thor's hammer.

When the Guardians are devising a plan to take the orb from Ronan, Quill claims to have "12%" of a plan. This is the same percentage of credit that Tony Stark was willing to concede to Pepper for the creation of Stark Tower in The Avengers.

Among Tivan's collection of species is a Chitauri soldier from the Avengers, and a Dark Elf from Thor: The Dark World.

There are two scenes after the movie finishes. The first one is of a young Groot dancing, with Drax trying to catch him out. The second scene comes right at the very end - Howard the Duck makes a cameo appearance with The Collector. Howard can also be seen faintly in the background of the scene with The Collector during the movie.

The dog that licks The Collector in the end credits scene is called Cosmo the Spacedog. Cosmo is actually a telepathic dog created by Dan Abnett and Andy Lanning, and appeared in the Marvel comics.

Laura Haddock, who plays Peter Quill's mother, had a small part in Captain America: The First Avenger, as a girl who asks for an autograph from Steve Rogers.

This isn't the first time Howard the duck has ended up in The Collectors exhibit, he can be seen in an episode of Hulk and the Agents of SMASH. He makes a cameo appearance in one of the pods of The Collector who admires the "ultra rare hero", stating he's in mint condition.

Troma Films creator Lloyd Kaufman has a brief cameo during

the prison sequence. He is seen among other inmates briefly looking over a railing. "Guardians" director James Gunn got his start with Troma and is good friends with Kaufman, hence the cameo.

Dave Bautista was driving to the gym when he got the call from his manager and agent to inform him he got the role of Drax. He was informed by being told "Congratulations, Mr. Drax." He claims that upon being informed, he broke down crying hysterically and had to go home, because he was so happy and awestruck by landing the role.

When Peter is about to kiss Gamora, behind them can be seen a window with a design inspired by Iron Man's arc reactor chest piece.

Director James Gunn's dog has a holographic cameo at the beginning of the film, while Star Lord is dancing.

Adam's Warlock's cocoon (also seen in Thor: The Dark World) and Eson the Searcher can be seen in the collector's place.

When Quill has been arrested on Xandar and his name and crimes are being reviewed, his alias is shown on the view screen but it appears as "space-lord" and not "star-lord." As ever, they've got his name wrong.

AVENGERS: AGE OF ULTRON MISTAKES

SPOILER - The wounds on Pietro's body change. The most noticeable one is on his right shoulder. The amount of blood decreases too.

Walt Disney Pictures

When Captain America is fighting Ultron in the truck, for a brief moment you can see a safety line holding actor Chris Evans as he's hanging on the side of the cab of the truck.

After the Scarlet Witch forces Banner to become Hulk, he goes berserk in Johannesburg, South Africa. A few minutes earlier they were near the ocean at a ship scrap yard. Johannesburg is many kilometres away from any ocean.

When the city takes off it is surrounded by land. However while it is flying it is suddenly over a large body of water, but when it crashes back to the ground it is over land again.

During the party, Natasha has just walked away after flirting with Banner. On the bar behind him is a glass of red cocktail next to a silver cocktail shaker. In all subsequent shots while Captain America is talking to Banner, the two have moved much closer together. (00:27:00)

Walt Disney Pictures

During the big chase on the streets of Seoul, Capt. America's shield starts out with a few scratches and smudges on it. Towards the end, these disappear.

When Scarlet Witch enters the fight, after Hawkeye's pep talk, there's a payphone booth to her right, several feet away. In shots of her fighting, the double doors are seen behind her. When Hawkeye nods at her, in the next shot of her, she is standing with the phone booth behind her. And then she's not near the phone booth when Hawkeye and Scarlet Witch start to leave.

At the end of the movie, when Captain America and Black Widow are walking towards the camera to train the new Avengers, the reflection of the cameraman's feet are seen on the glass railings in the back as they walk backwards shooting the actors.

AVENGERS: AGE OF ULTRON TRIVIA

When all the Avengers are attempting to lift Thor's hammer, Captain America is able to move it slightly. In the comics, Cap is one of the few characters noble enough to be able to lift Thor's hammer (notable others being Storm and Beta Ray Bill).

When Tony Stark is choosing FRIDAY as his AI companion, there's a card labeled JOCASTA. Jocasta, in the comics, is a robot, member of Avengers, and was created by Ultron.

Stan Lee makes his customary appearance whilst the Avengers and a load of War Veterans are enjoying a get together. Thor offers a 1,000 year old Asgardian drink to Captain America, and Stan Lee asks for some.

Walt Disney Pictures

Aaron Taylor-Johnson was apprehensive about joining the cast due to Marvel's intense contracts and schedules. Even after signing on, he was extremely nervous. It wasn't until he found out his character's twin sister was being played by Elizabeth Olsen that he calmed down and really got excited about the project, as they are close friends and had previously played husband and wife in 2014's "Godzilla."

Unlike previous movies in the Marvel franchise, there is only one credits extra, and that's in the middle, featuring Thanos and the Infinity Gauntlet.

Scarlett Johanasson was pregnant during filming, and thus had to rely on stunt-doubles moreso than usual. Amusingly, the three stunt-doubled hired to cover for her resembled her so greatly, the cast often would mistake the doubles for her and try to have conversations about the scenes and filming, only to realise they were talking to the "wrong" Black Widow.

Wakanda is the home country of Black Panther, another Marvel character, due to appear in Captain America: Civil War.

Near the end of the film, the Vision saves the Scarlet Witch, a possible foreshadowing of the beginning of their romantic relationship from the comics. These characters were married for a long time in the pages of the Avengers and even temporarily had children (it's complicated).

The innovation on Steve's arm, using a magnet for his shield, is a reference from Avengers Vol. 1 #006 from 1964.

Hawkeye's outfit is black and purple, those are his costume's colors in the comics.

Hawkeye's "Nobody would know" line was ad-libbed by Jeremy Renner.

When Vision says he's not Ultron or Jarvis, he simply says "I am." "I Am" is one of the names Jehovah/Jesus uses in the Bible.

The crimson cowl was used by Ultron in the Avengers #54 comic in 1968.

The SHIELD technician on board the Helicarrier at the end of the movie (who announces the lifeboats taking off) also appeared in Captain America: The Winter Soldier as the SHIELD agent who refused to send out the Insight Helicarriers and was threatened by Rumlow.

The Hulk does not have a single word of dialogue in the film.

The title does not appear until twelve minutes into the film.

Joss Whedon desperately wanted to have a surprise cameo by upcoming Marvel Cinematic Universe heroes Captain Marvel and especially Spider-Man (who he had just learned was going to be rejoining Marvel) during the final scene where we see the new Avengers assembling to train, but he was unable to for time and logistics reasons.

ANT-MAN MISTAKES

Twice in the film it is made clear that the Pym particle works by reducing the space between atoms in order to shrink an object, and by increasing it to enlarge them. This means that the object will weigh the same, whether shrunk or enlarged - it cannot be otherwise. A 90kg man the size of an ant would punch a hole through any surface upon which he stood (and couldn't ride ants), Doctor Pym has been walking about with a 60 tonne tank in his pocket, Darren Cross lifts a full grown sheep between finger and thumb, and the supersized Thomas The Tank Engine would be far too light to crush the police car (in fact it would float harmlessly away as it would probably weigh less than the air it displaced).

In order to enter the Pym Tech building, they drop the pressure in the water main and Scott floats in on a raft of fire ants. Getting into it the supply line would mean they have to enter from the municipal main, which would be under full pressure. Even with reduced pressure, the interior pipe would still be full of water. Additionally, Scott would not be able to enter through a faucet unless someone had left it running (the valve would be closed).

Cross is holding a normal striker fired (no external hammer) Glock handgun against the head of Ant-Man. In order to save his life, Hope orders the ants to block the firing mechanism of the gun, and they block a suddenly-visible hammer on the Glock. (01:26:00 - 01:27:00)

When Cross is on the model rail track, you see Thomas the tank engine fall off the track when he hits Cross. But in the next scene

Cross throws him from the track. (01:40:00)

In the water pipe scene, water pipes don't have printing on the inside of them. Bolt flanges are not inside pipes, and welds are not that close together, nor are the welds inside the pipe. Also how did he get to the faucet without someone turning on the water to that particular sink?

If the Pym Particle works by reducing the space between atoms to make an object smaller, the atoms themselves remain at normal size but are more closely packed together. It would, therefore, be impossible to "go subatomic" since the object obviously couldn't shrink and be smaller than the size of the atoms it was composed of.

When they are going over the plan for the last time at Pym's house a close up of Luis shows his top button undone, then the next close up it's done up, with no time to do it.

When Cross is seen inside Hank's home, he is wearing black gloves, a few moments later, in the same scene you can see that he is not wearing them anymore.

Disney/Marvel

Towards the end while Scott, Paxton and Cassie are eating, the steak on Cassie's plate moves between shots.

Scott Lang is swept out of the tub after having shrunk for the first time. When he lands on the ceramic bathroom floor, falling roughly two feet, there is an audible glass breaking sound and it appears he has broken the flooring with his fall. He then falls through a plaster ceiling to free fall down to a turntable, landing on a plastic vinyl record played by a DJ. The album does not break despite him having fallen from three times the height and landing on a weaker material. Moments later, he is thrown through a second storey window and lands on a car in the street and his weight is now once again sufficient to form a small dent in the hood. (00:31:15)

When Scott escapes from jail with the help of the ants, as he's flying through the trolley car he lands on a newspaper. From the position of the man's thumb, the picture is just a small part of the left side (his thumb lays over about half the width of the picture). When it cuts to the wide shot, the picture now covers more than half the page (width-wise).

When Scott uses the suit for the first time, he is on a tube with a small red towel on it which disappears between shots. Not only this - the amount of food on the plate reduces and then increases during the scene.

When going subatomic, Scott passes into an atom. The image shown is of the Rutherford model of the atom with electrons orbiting the nucleus. This model is incorrect and has been replaced with the more-accurate Bohr model of the atom.

When Scott wakes up after falling off Anthony, we can see the floor around the bed and there are no ants there. He then looks down and sees the bed is surrounded by ants.

Ant-Man is riding carpenter ants after a helicopter in flight. The ants are coming at the helicopter from under it as it rises off the helipad. This wouldn't be possible due to the down force of air from the rotors. (01:30:00)

After getting fired from Baskin-Robbins, Scott goes "home" to the Milgrom Hotel. As he approaches, there is a bicycle chained to a parking meter in front of the hotel; it is also visible in the close shot through the gate from inside. In the long inside shot from down the hall as Scott actually enters, the bike is gone.

As they are heading back to the city, the scene switches back and forth from Luis to Scott. There is nothing but shrubbery visible through the window to Scott's right, but suddenly, there are two cuts in which they appear to be very close to an unidentified bridge. The closing shot on the scene shows the bridge to still be way off in the distance. The bridge would not have been off to their right if they were still approaching from the north.

Near the end, Scott Lang inadvertently shrinks to subatomic size, drifting through a kaleidoscopic quantum universe, and we see him reacting to the visual effects. However, at subatomic size, Scott shouldn't be able to "see" anything, because the rods and cones in the human retina can only "see" in a narrow band of light frequencies, and Scott is far, far smaller than the frequency of visible light waves. Additionally, Scott couldn't possibly "hear" his daughter Cassie crying "Where are you, Daddy?" Human hearing is based completely on air vibrations at certain frequencies, and Scott is millions of times smaller than sonic frequencies or even the nearest air molecule.

Near the start of the movie, Darren Cross is showing the Yellowjacket armour to a group of some visitors. One person, named Frank begins talking with Cross about the armour. There is one shot shown during the talk, with the camera behind Frank's shoulder. In the shot, Frank is heard talking but his jaw is not shown moving along with the line.

Scott's stubble changes dramatically in three consecutive scenes - when his boss sacks him it is quite pronounced, but on his way home it is much lighter, and when he enters the apartment it is back to full-on stubble again.

ANT-MAN TRIVIA

The Burig uniform and linen is a reference to Susan A. Burig, the graphic designer of this film.

At Baskin Robbins Paul Rudd is wearing a badge with the name "Jack" - a reference to Jack Kirby, a co-creator of Ant-Man.

One of Cross' henchmen has a ten rings tattoo, a reference to the Mandarin from Iron Man 3.

Several costumes were made, all identical. The ones worn by Paul Rudd when he is standing talking and walking were made of many different metal parts and leather. The stunt suits were all made of foam rubber so all metal belts, straps were one piece instead of metal interlocking pieces. 17 different helmets were made of metal and again foam rubber, also ones that were open at the front so we can see the face, some fitted with yellow lenses and ones fitted without. Once Paul Rudd was wearing the helmet the chin strap was added and screwed into position. The stunt helmet was foam rubber and simply worn on his head - it was pull on / pull off in case of injury.

When Scott first shrinks, one of the things he encounters is a Kirby brand vacuum cleaner. Jack Kirby was one of the co-creators of Ant-Man.

In the Pym house there is a red small chair, that's the very first object shrunk by Ant-Man in the comics.

Garrett Morris makes a cameo as the man in the car when Scott hits its roof. Morris was the first person to portray Ant-Man in a

1979 sketch for Saturday Night Live called Superhero Party.

Disney/Marvel

The yellowjacket's plasma cannons sound exactly like the AT-

AT from The Empire Strikes Back.

Director Peyton Reed was up for consideration as one of the directors of last year's Guardians of the Galaxy, but that project was ultimately given to James Gunn. However, Reed was not forgotten - after Edgar Wright had exited the Ant-Man project, Peyton Reed was then given the opportunity to direct Ant-Man.

Stan lee makes his usual cameo before the end as the bartender who talks with Ignacio.

There is a post credits scene where the new Wasp costume is shown.

Mitchell Carson (who gets punched) in the comics was going to wear the Ant-Man suit for SHIELD, but it was taken by Eric O'Grady, who became the fourth Ant-Man.

Yellowjacket was another identity used by Hank Pym in the comics.

While denying the rumored existence of an Ant-Man, Darren Cross uses the phrase "Tales to Astonish." Ant-Man's first appearance in a Marvel comic form was under the title Tales to Astonish #27 (January 1962).

In the final scene, Luis is talking with Scott about his friend's date who met up with The Falcon one time. Luis stated that The Falcon was asking that he is looking for a guy and the woman talks about the guys she knows. One of the guys Luis said she mentioned is a guy who climbs walls. This is a clear reference to Spider-Man, who is set to appear in the Marvel Cinematic Universe very soon.

There is at the very end a post credits scene where Captain America and Falcon are talking with the Winter Soldier.

CAPTAIN AMERICA: CIVIL WAR MISTAKES

In the first Avengers briefing with the Secretary, the shot has Tony Stark sitting in the back with a wedding ring on. The shot changes to another view and Tony is sitting in the same location, but is no longer wearing a wedding ring. This continues many times within the scene.

When Spidey takes Cap's shield he uses his web on it, but when he lands on the car the web on the shield is gone.

Walt Disney Pictures

When the winter soldier is getting away from the police in Bucharest he jumps to the next building and the sun is shining directly onto the ground. When he lands the sun has suddenly shifted and the shadow of the other building is visible.

While Black Widow fights the two bad guys before the drone retrieves the biohazard capsule, the sun changes between shots.

As Captain America arrives in his car at the airport car park, he stops right next to the line dividing the spots. In the following shot, when he steps out, the car is further away from the line, more towards the center of the spot. (01:26:50)

During the face-off between Bucky, Captain America and Iron Man at the end of the film the fake snow is seen stuck to the actors after they fall down. It remains throughout the scene rather than melting as real snow would.

When Steve jumps onto the police truck and breaks the windshield, the glass is slightly cracked, but when Cap takes out the whole windshield it's completely smashed.

After Falcon's drone shoots the man with the vial, it begins to fall to the ground and Black Widow catches it. In the close-up shot, the lid is in the palm of her hand, but when she gets up the vial has turned around, with the lid now above her hand. (00:11:00)

Walt Disney Pictures

The wound on Black Panther's left eyebrow disappears at the end of the film.

While the sink is filling in the interrogation scene, the water is running over his shoulder, however when the camera shifts above, the faucet is not close enough to have water running over him. (00:25:00 - 00:27:00)

While Cap is fighting Crossbones, the items on the table behind them change between shots.

At the end of the film when they are fighting in the chambers, Captain America destroys the right boot thruster. Later, they say it is the left, and the right one is fine. (02:04:15 - 02:05:30)

Shortly before the EMP bomb is activated, the crate containing it is shown. "Diese Seite Oben" is painted on the box, which is a bad translation of "This side up." In Germany crates only use the word "oben" to indicate the upper side of a box.

At the beginning when Crossbones and the others are about to enter the hospital the sun changes between shots.

When Bucky is escaping, Black Panther is behind and below him, but in the next shot he reappears in front of him.

CAPTAIN AMERICA: CIVIL WAR TRIVIA

In the film Falcon uses a drone named Redwing. In the comics he uses a real falcon with the same name.

When the film was first announced, it was jokingly called "Captain America: Serpent Society" before its actual title was revealed a few minutes later.

There is an extra post-credits sequence with Spiderman.

At the age of 19, Tom Holland is the youngest actor to play Spider-Man/Peter Parker on the big screen.

The directors have previously worked on both Community and Arrested Development - both shows get nods in this movie. Jim Rash, the Dean from Community, plays an MIT faculty member at the start. More subtle is the Bluth family's stair-car from Arrested Development, seen briefly as Captain America walks onto the airport runway before the big battle with the other Avengers.

The girl on her cell phone in Peter's hallway is Sophia Russo, director Joe Russo's daughter.

Director Joe Russo appears in the film as Dr. Broussard, the murdered psychiatrist hired to interview Bucky. Russo plays a different character than he did in "Captain America: Winter Soldier", but still uses the alias Gozie Agbo in the credits.

In the comics, a group of celebrity superhuman vigilantes tried to take down a house of super-villains on television, but one of the villains escaped due to the vigilante's incompetence and blew up a school, killing hundreds of children. At the memorial, which Stark attended, a woman accused him of letting it happen (although he had nothing to do with it), leading him to support the act so that such reckless acts of heroism would not happen again.

Stan Lee makes a cameo at the end of the movie as the FedEx man who says "Are you Tony Stank?"

After Tony blows off Bucky's arm, Cap picks up his shield and shields himself from Tony's blasts. At the very end of the shot, Tony is firing a beam at Cap which lands on Cap's shield and the shot begins to slow down. This moment from the shot is an homage to the cover from part 7 of the Marvel Civil War comic storyline, where Captain America and Iron Man are fighting on the front cover in the same way.

Walt Disney Pictures

In the comics Tony Stark and Reed Richards worked to design a superhuman prison known as Prison 42, which was made specifically for super humans who disobeyed the Registration Act. It was top secret and was used to hold many of those on Team Cap about halfway through the arc. Captain America later broke his teammates out of the prison.

When Tony Stark is visiting the Raft, an imprisoned Clint Barton mockingly calls him a "futurist." In 2004, Robert Downey Jr. released an album called "The Futurist."

Sharon Carter says a eulogy at her aunt Peggy's funeral, with the quote from Peggy, "your job is to plant yourself like a tree and say no, you move." This line is actually an iconic quote from the newer Captain America comics, and is said by Captain America, not Peggy Carter. The quote was said in Amazing Spider-Man #237, published in 2007.

While the accident in the film that kicks off the Civil War is the explosion in Wakanda, in the comics, the disaster was a villain named Nitro who exploded near an American school. Tony was also confronted at a memorial rather than a university convention.

DOCTOR STRANGE MISTAKES

In the first scene where Dr Strange is preparing for surgery he uses improper surgical gowning technique breaking aseptic protocols. Strange puts on a mask after washing his hands, contaminating his clean hands by bringing them in proximity to the non-sterile environment of his face. Surgical masks must be worn before the full washing of hands. Another error is that he inserted his hands all the way through his gown to don gloves. Hands must never leave the sleeves and gloves must be put on with the sleeves still covering.

Strange is at home, looking for help on a video chat. His friend says no, and in his rage he sweeps almost everything off the table including the Microsoft Surface laptop. Christine enters with food, we cut back, and the area of the table to his left, which was totally clear a second ago, now has several pieces of paper on it and the laptop with a closed lid. A few moments and cuts later, the laptop is in perfect condition on the table with the lid open.

After Doctor Strange experiments with the magical doorway in the Sanctum Sanctorum, he leaves it on a desert view and we cut to a shot panning across all the artifacts. At the very start of the shot on the right hand side of the screen is a crewmember standing in the shadows looking bored. Really blatant if you turn up the brightness, but easy enough to spot if you know what you're looking at. (00:56:00)

Walt Disney Pictures

When he rushes a patient to brain surgery they show him and the other doctor operating without surgical masks. When they cut away and come back they're wearing masks. Also, the doctor that is assisting him is an ER doctor, that would never happen in real life.

When Tilda Swinton dies and is lying on the operating table, her pupils are not dilated as they would be immediately after death.

When Hong Kong is being destroyed, a vendor's sign falls to the ground, written in English. However, in the shot where the city is being restored, the same sign is now in Chinese.

The wound and blood on Strange's left eyebrow is first fresh, then dry, then it's gone, then is back again.

When Kaecilius is attached to a wall just his hand is free, but in the next shot now his head and other hand are free too.

DOCTOR STRANGE TRIVIA

The sorcerors' WiFi password, Shamballa, is a reference to the 1986 Doctor Strange graphic novel "Into Shamballa."

The envelope opened by Strange has the same year of birth as the release of Doctor Strange Vol. 2 #1 in 1974.

In Stan Lee's cameo he is reading The Doors of Perception by Aldous Huxley, a book about the author's experience of taking the mind altering psychotropic mescaline.

Mid credits scene: Thor pays a visit to Strange to help with Loki and find Odin. This scene takes place in the upcoming 2017 Marvel film Thor: Ragnarok.

There is a post credit scene that shows Mordo stealing Pangborn's magic.

There are 2 credit scenes, one in the middle and one right at the end.

When Dr Strange experiments with the forbidden Eye of Agamotto and time spells in the Book of Cagliostro, he uses an apple to practice on. Apples symbolically represent Forbidden Knowledge.

Chiwetel Ejiofor was already a black belt in karate before taking the role.

Tilda Swinton's children worked on the film crew - her daughter worked in the costume department and her son in the art department.

Joaquin Phoenix was also in the running to play Doctor Strange but turned down the role as he didn't want to sign a multi-picture contract with the studio.

Dan Harmon, creator of the cult-favorite series "Community" and "Rick and Morty," was brought on to help fine-tune the film during post production by giving notes on the editing. He also helped re-write several scenes during reshoots.

Rachel McAdams' reaction to the mop falling in the closet after Doctor Strange leaves back through the portal is genuine. The camera was still rolling when the mop fell over on its own, scaring McAdams. The director liked it so much he kept it in the movie.

Stan Lee's cameo is as a passenger on a bus that Doctor Strange slams into.

The Mirror Dimension special effects were influenced by the art of M.C. Escher, and by fractal shapes.

The shot of the paper with Strange's multiple attempts to sign his name is very similar to Strange: Beginnings and endings, 2005.

The footage of Strange flying in the realm space is like in Strange Tales Vol. 1 #138 from 1965.

The film was shot partly in Nepal, with exterior scenes in several Kathmandu locations including Pashupati, home of Pashupatinath Temple, and Lalitpur's Patan Durbar Square, a unesco World Heritage site. The interiors of Kamar-Taj were created on a soundstage in London.

While Strange and the bad guys are fighting around the city the Synchrony bank can be seen. This is Marvel's official bank, sponsor of their Mastercards.

When Strange's soul comes out of his body it's similar to Doctor Strange: The Oath #1 from 2006.

GUARDIANS OF THE GALAXY VOL. 2 MISTAKES

During the opening scene with Ego and Quill's mother, they run into the woods behind the Dairy Queen, and mom is wearing boots with fur trim. When they get to where the Ego's plant is in the ground, she is suddenly wearing sandals.

In the beginning of the movie when the guardians are getting ready to fight off an interdimensional being Rocket winks a couple of times at Starlord. Starlord then responds but is looking to his left at Rocket, whilst Rocket is on his right side. The scene is for no reason mirrored, proven by the big orange device behind him also switching from being on his left to on his right. (00:03:45)

In the scene early in the movie where Kurt Russell and Star Lord's mother walk in the woods behind the Dairy Queen, she has on boots with fur tops as they walk down the hill, and has sandals on while standing in the clearing near the god plant.

When Taserface is threatening Rocket, Rocket is making eye contact. Taserface, meanwhile, is looking at the space between Rocket's ears.

At the very beginning of the film it says that it's 1980 Missouri with a nuclear power plant in the background. The plant in the film has 4 cooling towers, but the only nuclear plant in Missouri (Callaway Nuclear Generating Station) has only one cooling tower and it didn't begin operation until 1984.

While Yondu is explaining how he tracked the Milano, and who sent him and why, look at the 3 arrows pinned to Yondu's jacket when he first appears. Once he starts his walk around while explaining, there are only 2 arrows. After the scene returns from Nebula and baby Groot, the shot seems to be mirrored, with the three arrows in a different position. (00:40:15)

GUARDIANS OF THE GALAXY VOL. 2 TRIVIA

Vin Diesel was given a special "Groot" version of the script that contained "translations" of what Groot was actually saying whenever he utters his one and only repeated sentence "I am Groot." This was done to help him deliver his dialog appropriately, since he would know exactly what point Groot was trying to get across with each line. Reportedly, only Diesel was given this version of the script - in everyone else's script, Groot's dialog is merely "I am Groot" over and over again.

During the end credits, "I am Groot" appears throughout. The phrase will then shift to reveal the "translation", usually someone's name.

David Bowie was intended to have a cameo in the film, but tragically passed away before a deal could be reached.

James Gunn's parents, James Sr. And Leota, make cameos in the film as "Weird Old Man" and "Weird Old Man's Mistress."

SPOILER: Stan Lee's cameo shows him discussing his time as a FedEx employee (a nod to his cameo from "Captain America: Civil War") and presumably his exploits from other MCU films to a group of large bald humanoid beings. These beings are known as Watchers, who are an alien race whose sole purpose is to observe events throughout the universe. This is in keeping with a fan theory that Stan Lee's cameos within the MCU (and possibly Marvel films that are not part of the MCU) point to him being a Watcher himself, or at least someone that reports to them as this film would suggest.

The wide-shots that show the entirety of Ego the living planet are actually some of the most complex visual effects shots ever, at least in terms of size and scope. One VFX artist has stated that the digital model is about equal to a polygon count of close to one trillion, as they added as much detail as was possible.

During one of the mid-credits scenes, we see Sylvester Stallone assembling a team of old ravager buddies. The member that is a disembodied head ("Mainframe") is actually voiced by talented-but-controversial singer Miley Cyrus in an uncredited cameo. Director James Gunn thought her unique sense of spunk and energy lent itself well to the character.

Spoiler. Writer/Director James Gunn spent months trying to figure out a way to end the film without killing off the character Yondu, as Yondu's actor Michael Rooker was a close friend of his and he wanted the character to be in the planned third film. But he ultimately decided that Yondu's redemption and self-sacrifice to save his surrogate "son" Peter was far too important to the theme of fatherhood in the film, and went ahead with killing off the character. Rooker was a bit crestfallen at first when he found out about his character's death, but ultimately agreed with Gunn's decision.

SPOILER: During the second mid-credits scene, we see Stakar regrouping with some of his old Ravager buddies. These characters (Krugarr, Aleta, Charlie-27, Martinex, and Mainframe) along with Yondu were the original Guardians of the Galaxy team in the comics.

The 80's Sony Walkman and headphones seen in the film were built from scratch, as the ones used in the original film were somehow lost and the production had a great deal of trouble finding real ones that worked for a reasonable price. As they hadn't been produced in close to 30 years, it ended up being cheaper and easier for the prop team to just build close approximations.

Howard the duck makes a small cameo on one of the planets.

SPOILER: During the third mid-credits scene, we see the high priestess Ayesha reveal that she is creating a being to destroy the Guardians, and that she will call him Adam. This is Adam Warlock, who in the comics is a being that was genetically engineered to be perfect and is Ayesha's "brother." He also played a very important role in the "Infinity Gauntlet" and "Infinity War" comic book storylines that the next "Avengers" films were based on, although the character didn't appear in the movies.

When Nebula and Gamora come across the skulls, one of the skulls has a horse-like shape to it. This is a reference to the character Beta Ray Bill, who in the comics was one of few characters worthy enough to lift Thor's hammer. Or possibly Kymellians - horse headed aliens closely associated with the preteen Marvel team, Power Pack.

Jeff Goldblum makes an appearance as the Grandmaster during the credits. You can see him dancing in the sidecards along with the other Guardians after the mid-credits scene with the Sovereign High Priestess. This marked Goldblum's first appearance as the character, six full months before he was featured in "Thor: Ragnarok."

SPIDER-MAN: HOMECOMING MISTAKES

When the bus is shown entering Washington, DC for the competition, the shot shows the bus traveling over the Arlington Memorial Bridge with the Lincoln Memorial in the background. That bridge is on the southwest side of the city. Since NYC is to the northeast of DC, this means that to get to that bridge and enter DC that way, the bus had to drive all the way around the city and then come back in from the opposite direction. Even if the bus driver made a mistake and missed the most direct route into the city from the north, there are dozens of other ways to get to the heart of the city without adding a good 45 minutes to an hour to the trip.

The ferry splits in half down the middle, enough so the water is flooding in dramatically as the split grows. There is no possible way that the two halves of the ferry could have remained afloat like that. It would have sunk immediately. Then, as Iron Man "welds" the two halves back together, the ferry is afloat at the same waterline as before the incident, certainly not feasible with all the water it took on.

After Toomes and his crew lose the cleanup contract and they are back in their shop, on the table is a Coors "stubby" Banquet beer bottle. This bottle was released in 2013 and the scene takes place earlier than that.

When Spidey first interrupts the criminals on the ferry, there are 2 motorbikes behind him on the left. When he throws one of the bad guys around with a web, the bikes have moved to the right, along with the yellow markings they were on, showing the shot's been flipped. They then move back.

Sony Pictures

In Peter's personal vlog of the airport battle from Civil War, he jumps in, grabs Cap's shield and immediately says "hey everyone." However, in Civil War he jumps in and grabs the shield without saying anything, Tony says "nice job, kid", there's a longer chat about the suit, and only later does Spider-Man say "hey everyone."

When Ant-Man goes giant during the airport fight in Civil War, Peter is out in the airfield and reacts with a surprised "holy shit!" His video diary in Homecoming instead shows Peter hiding away from the action, and he reacts to the moment with a more subdued "aw crap, he's big, I gotta go now."

After Peter gets the text from Happy about meeting at the bathroom, Michelle asks, "What are you hiding, Peter?" and just as she says, "I'm just kidding I don't care," Peter's holding his cell phone up in his left hand, but next shot he's holding the cell phone up in his right hand.

Sony Pictures

When Spider-Man stops the "Avengers" from robbing the ATM, there's a car parked outside at the start, visible through the window, which disappears a few seconds later, and then reappears after that.

Sony Pictures

When the ferry starts splitting in two, there are people standing at the back and cars on the bottom. In a wide shot the people and cars have disappeared, then the people reappear a few seconds later, as do the cars in a later shot.

Sony Pictures

When Spidey falls into the elevator, there is a bag that disappears, reappears, and even moves to the side between shots.

When Spidey saves Liz from falling off the Washington Monument, he shoots some web on her hand and wrist which disappears a few shots later.

When Spidey falls into the water he is trapped in the parachute then the armour takes him out and the parachute is gone.

Near the start of the movie, Peter Parker is doing sit ups assisted by his friend. As the camera moves left, Peter is seen doing the exercise with both hands behind his head but as the camera then moves to a different angle he has both arms crossed over his chest with his hands at his shoulders.

When Spider-Man is at the top of the Washington Monument, in the background we can see a sniper aiming straight at him from the helicopter. We cut to a closer shot of the chopper, and the guy's rifle is suddenly lowered, then he raises it.

Sony Pictures

Spidey left his backpack attached to a trash bin. Later he gets it back but the alley is different.

When the Vulture gets into the damage control truck he grabs some items from there and puts them in a bag. He didn't have the bag before he jumped in.

When Peter breaks the door of the damage control truck, the black bag behind him disappears and reappears between shots.

A poster in the school states that the Academic Decathlon takes place on October 14-15. But later on in the movie, another poster says it's on September 14.

While Peter is doing crunches with Ned his hands change positions between shots.

When Peter Parker leaves homecoming and finds Michael Keaton in the warehouse, at one point the engine is swinging in the crane, the camera cuts away and comes back and the engine is perfectly still.

SPIDER-MAN: HOMECOMING TRIVIA

Jennifer Connelly voices the "suit lady", the AI in Spider-Man's suit. In real life she's married to Paul Bettany, who voiced Jarvis, the AI in Iron Man's suit, and who later played Vision.

Principal Morita of the school is a descendent of Jim Morita, seen in action in Captain America: The First Avenger. He also has a photo of him in his office.

When Spidey sits on a lamp post, behind him on a wall there is graffiti with the name "Bagley" on it - that's a reference to the Ultimate Spider-Man artist Mark Bagley.

Stan Lee makes a cameo as the guy who speaks with a lady from building to building.

Tony Revolori received death threats after he was cast in the role of Flash Thompson.

Longtime actor Michael Keaton seems permanently attached to winged superhero roles. Keaton began the superhero phase of his career in 1989 as "Batman" in the original film and its first sequel. Keaton was nominated for an Academy Award for 2014's "Birdman," playing a washed-up actor who was once a flying superhero movie star. In "Spiderman: Homecoming," Keaton plays the high-flying villain Adrian Toomes (aka "Vulture").

Michelle has the same personality as Gwen Stacy from Marvel's Ultimate Universe.

The license plate on Shocker's van is MAR4667, that's a reference to Amazing Spider-Man #46 from March 1967 which was his first appearance.

The scene where Peter is trapped under the rubble of Vulture's lair and uses his spider strength to lift the concrete off himself and escape is a recreation of a famous scene from Amazing Spider-Man #33.

The gauntlets used by the shocker are an upgrade of those used by Crossbones in Captain America: Civil War.

There is a mid credit scene with Toomes speaking with another villain.

When Happy is getting Stark's stuff on the plane, the Mark 42 armor from Iron Man 3 can be seen.

In Peter's room there are two flags of the New York Mets. Peter is a huge fan of that baseball team in the comics.

While Spidey drives Flash's car, in the background there is graffiti with "McFarlane" on it as reference to Todd McFarlane, another comic artist.

There is a post credit scene with Captain America.

Adrian Toomes is never referred to as "The Vulture" in the movie.

The homemade suit of Spidey is inspired by the Scarlet Spider suit from the comics.

The license plate on aunt May's car has AMF1562 on it, a reference to Amazing Fantasy #15 from 1962.

In the science lab on the front wall there is a photo of Bruce Banner.

During an appearance on "The Chef Show," Gwyneth Paltrow revealed to Jon Favreau that she had no idea she appeared in this movie. Given how secretive Marvel is about their film productions, she most likely thought the scene she was filming was for an Avengers movie.

THOR: RAGNAROK MISTAKES

When Karl Urban is defending the Asgardians, the dust covers on his rifles vary between being open and closed several times. M16 dust covers are sprung loaded - they open on the first shot and have to be manually closed afterwards.

When Thor speaks with Valkyrie in Hulk's room, he makes his presence known by leaning on the end of one of the drinks racks. But in the following shot, he's moved a few steps back. (01:10:20)

When Thor and Loki are in front of the Shady Acres care home, an old man wearing a black hat passes behind them but in the next shot a woman is there instead.

During the fight in the forest with Heimdall and Hela's soldiers, he uses the sword but the tree is cut before the hit, and the soldiers on the right fall before the hit too.

Banner is covered in green powder, but when he is separated from Thor the powder covering his face and hair is suddenly gone.

When Valkyrie is drinking and watching the fight between Thor and Hulk, an object appears in her hands from nowhere.

When Loki gets up from being thrown during the "get help" scene, he seems too far to the left of the screen (Thor's right). Thor is still looking down to his left at the fallen guards, and in the previous shot we saw that Loki fell amongst them as he knocked them down.

Hela kicks Hogun and breaks the wall, but a few shots later he is standing in the middle of the square.

In the scene when the Hulk is changing back into Bruce, he is wearing a round plated metal belt around his waist. But straight after when Bruce is lying on the floor there is no belt, just the material.

After Hela breaks the hammer she has a sword in her left hand which disappears in the next shot.

After pardoning his cousin with the melt stick, when he says "I'm stepping in it" Topaz can be seen with the melting stick on her left, in the next shot she has it in her right and then back to her left hand when she says "burnt toast." (00:39:00)

According to the previous film, Thor: The Dark World, Asgardian kings live approximately 5,000 years. (If I want to be cautious here, this statement is only valid about Odin and of unknown validity about other Asgardians.) But in this film, Thor says Odin fought Surtur 500,000 years before.

When Thor pats Loki's back, he's placing the electrical chip that he will later use to zap him. It's about waist-high. When he zaps him, it's much higher, closer to his shoulders.

THOR: RAGNAROK TRIVIA

Stan Lee makes his usual cameo as the guy that cuts Thor's hair.

When Thor is strapped in the chair we can hear the music from the original Charlie and the Chocolate Factory; specifically an instrumental version of Pure Imagination.

Spoiler! There is a mid credit scene that features Thanos' ship.

The helmet used by Thor is very similar to the classic helmet used by him in the comics.

A Make A Wish child who visited the set suggested Thor's "friend from work" line about the Hulk to Chris Hemsworth.

Spoiler - Thor takes the Asgard people in a spaceship, like Beta Ray Bill did in the comics.

Cate Blanchett chose to do the movie for her children who are Marvel comics fans. Her eldest son suggested she play Hela as a career boost.

Taika Waititi said "I would say we improvised probably eighty percent of the film, or ad-libbed and threw in stuff" in an MTV news interview.

In order to keep a light yet collaborative mood amongst the cast on set, around 80 per cent of the dialogue in the movie was improvised.

Anthony Hopkins originally didn't intend to return for this film, but upon reading the script, he changed his mind.

Cate Blanchett studied Capoeira (an Afro-Brazilian martial art) for her role as Hela.

Chris Hemsworth bulked up to play Thor by working out 6-7 times a week and eating 6000 calories a day of a strict selection of foods.

Led Zeppelin's 'Immigrant Song' was chosen for the soundtrack because the lyrics mention Norse mythology.

AVENGERS: INFINITY WAR MISTAKES

On the spaceship, Peter is talking to Tony, and has his hair swept back with gel or similar. When he says "You can't be a friendly neighbourhood Spider-Man if there's no neighbourhood", we cut to Tony then back, and Peter now has a fringe with no gel. In later shots it's back how it was before.

When Doctor Strange attempts to use the Time Stone on Ebony Maw, Maw ties up Doctor Strange telepathically and strangles him unconscious. Beside Doctor Strange is a police car and a motorbike tipped on its side. Maw then lifts the ground Doctor Strange is lying on, but the police car has been replaced by an SUV and the motorbike has disappeared. The shadows also change. (00:23:25)

Walt Disney Pictures

When Thanos brings Vision back to life using the Time Stone, Thanos is standing a couple steps away from him after bringing him back. Wanda then tries to stop him, and it cuts to a wide shot where he suddenly is a couple of steps closer with his hand suddenly around Vision's neck. Thanos then pushes her with his other hand and in the next shot, Thanos is then reaching to put his hand around Vision's neck even though he was just shown with his hand around Vision's neck already. (02:09:35)

When Tony is talking with Pepper, she unties Tony's sleeves from around his shoulders when she points out the unit on his chest. The sleeves are hanging over Tony's shoulders in the wide shot as he says, "I'm just trying to protect us," but when it cuts to the closeup the sleeves have vanished, between shots. (00:12:20)

When Groot creates a handle for the axe with his arm, he chops off the arm and it lands on the ground. The sharp end is facing to the right when it lands, but when it begins to lift, the sharp end is now facing to the left. (01:44:20)

Walt Disney Pictures

Thanos' ship is near the ground in New York but seconds later when Peter senses it, the ship is higher, at building level. (00:18:10)

In New York after Bruce tries to become Hulk, in one shot there's a minor mud stain on his shirt, then the angle changes and it's suddenly a massive brown splat. (00:22:15)

Walt Disney Pictures

In the flashback to Gamora's planet while Thanos is walking beside Gamora, Ebony Maw disappears in the open view. (00:43:20)

Thor calls Nidavellir "Nivadellir" the first two times he mentions it.

Peter sneaks off the bus using the emergency exit window, which would have triggered an alarm when he released the red safety latch, ruining his stealthy escape.

The blanket used by Thor on the Guardians' ship moves several times between shots. (00:32:55)

When Peter sees the ship whilst he is on the school bus, he taps Ned on the shoulder and asks him to make a distraction. When he taps Ned on the shoulder, Ned has earphones in both ears, and one of the earphones falls out when Peter taps him, whilst the other earphone remains in his ear. But in the next shot, neither of his ears has an earphone in them. (00:18:25)

Walt Disney Pictures

Just after Proxima Midnight and Corvus Glaive land in the train station, there is a wide shot where they begin approaching Wanda and Vision. In the wide shot, their shadows do not appear to match up with each other, despite being under the same lighting. Proxima Midnight's shadow is positioned in front of her and is quite heavy, but Corvus Glaive's shadow is positioned more to his left and is much lighter than Proxima's.(00:40:20)

Walt Disney Pictures

When Thanos hits Wanda he is grabbing Vision by the neck, but in the next shot he grabs him again.

When Ebony Maw walks past the dead Asgardians, Corvus Glaive walks past him with his spear upright then the other way up. The spikes on the spear change shape too.

On Titan, when Tony begins speaking with Spider-Man, Star-Lord, Drax and Mantis, in the shot where he says "We gotta coalesce", Spider-Man is standing a few feet away from Tony and is facing him, but in the next shot, Spider-Man is suddenly standing closer to Tony and is now facing the others. (01:22:50)

When Ebony Maw is walking past the dead Asgardians, the camera pans from feet up to his face, and Corvus Glaive is walking past him. The shot cuts to a different angle, where Corvus Glaive is now several meters away from him. (00:01:35)

Walt Disney Pictures

When Heimdall is stabbed the sword gets into his chest around his heart, in the next scene they take the sword away from closer to his stomach.

When Loki reveals the Tesseract to Thanos, the first shot shows him holding it against his fingertips raised above his palm, but when Thor tells Loki he really is the worst brother, the Tesseract is now being held in his palm. Also, when Thanos tells Loki his optimism is misplaced, the Tesseract is still being held in his palm, but when the shot cuts, it is now being held against his fingertips raised slightly above his palm. (00:03:45)

Thor says "You talk too much" whilst Thanos has his hand grabbing Thor's head. Thanos' fingers are close together on one side, with his thumb holding the other side. Two shots after, when Thanos asks Loki for the Tesseract, Thanos' fingers are spread apart. Two shots after that, when Thanos says "Or your brother's head", his fingers are suddenly close together again. (00:02:55)

Walt Disney Pictures

AVENGERS: INFINITY WAR TRIVIA

Spoilers! Red Skull makes his long-awaited return to the MCU after his appearance in Captain America: The First Avenger. We discover that he's been guarding the soul stone as punishment, of sorts. However he's played by Ross Marquand, not Hugo Weaving.

Kenneth Branagh, director of the first Thor movie, has an audio cameo. He's the one voicing the distress call from the Asgardians which the Guardians of the Galaxy pick up.

In this film, Thanos' plan to wipe out half of all sentient life stems from his desire to bring balance to the universe. In the comics, he is motivated by his unrequited love for the physical embodiment of Death.

Spoiler! Whilst Groot is turning to dust after Thanos activates the complete Infinity Gauntlet, he says "I am Groot" to Rocket just before he dies. James Gunn, writer/director of the Guardians of the Galaxy movies, confirmed via Twitter that Groot was actually saying "Dad" to Rocket before dying.

The way Spidey hits Thanos and throws the web on his face is the same way he does in The Infinity Gauntlet comic book.

On Knowhere, Thanos is questioning The Collector, played by Benicio Del Toro, for the location of the Reality Stone. He asks him "Where is the stone?" at one point. This is a reference to a heist scene from the movie Snatch, in which Benicio Del Toro is robbing a bank and asks "Where is the stone?" with the same line intonation.

When Tony Stark blows Ebony Maw out of an opened gap, you can hear the Wilhelm scream.

There is a post credit scene where Nick Fury contacts Captain Marvel.

Will be released April 27, 2018. This is almost exactly ten years after the release of "Iron Man", the first entry in the "Marvel Cinematic Universe", which was released May 2, 2008.

The spider armour worn by Peter is very similar to the one Stark gives to Spidey in the comics "The spider bot".

(SPOILERS) As a result of the shocking twist ending where half of the peoples of the universe disintegrate into nothing, Reddit organized a huge campaign where they would ban half the subscribers of the subreddit /r/thanosdidnothingwrong to answer the question "Who would survive if this actually happened and who wouldn't?" Directors Joe and Anthony Russo also signed up for the campaign. At the end of the campaign, over 300,000 people had their accounts banned, including Joe Russo.

Despite its namesake, this film is based more on Marvel's "Infinity Gauntlet" storyline than it is "Infinity War." The latter storyline actually featured many of Marvel's heroes teaming up with Thanos to defeat a villain called the Magus.

The look of Black Widow with the white hair is a reference to Yelena Belova, a spy in the comics and second modern-era character to use the name Black Widow. She first appeared in Inhumans #5 in March 1999.

Red Skull calls Thanos "son of A'lars" aka Mentor. This character first appeared in Iron Man vol. 1 #55, and is the father of Thanos and Starfox.

"Avengers: Infinity War" holds several prestigious box-office records. Among others, it has the highest ever domestic opening weekend (at $257.6 million), the highest worldwide gross for a comic-book movie (at just over $2 billion as of 6/12/18), and is the fastest movie to gross $1 billion globally, reaching the number in just 11 days of release. It is also the only film ever released during the Summer movie season to hit $2 billion globally, and one of only four movies to ever reach the $2 billion mark. (The three others were holiday releases).

At the end Thanos uses his armour as a scarecrow, as in the comics.

Stan Lee makes his customary appearance, this time as the school bus driver.

When Thanos is battling the Guardians in the Collector's lair, he turns Drax into a bunch of cubes and Mantis into ribbons. He does the same thing in the "Infinity Gauntlet" storyline to his brother Starfox and Nebula, respectively.

The scales under Cap's suit reference the original suit in the comics.

Doctor Strange learns of the coming of Thanos after Hulk/Bruce Banner crash lands into the Sanctum Sanctorum and informs Strange of the looming threat. This is taken straight from the "Infinity Gauntlet" storyline, though there it is Silver Surfer that warns Doctor Strange.

BLACK PANTHER MISTAKES

When Klaue is being rescued by Erik, the amount of blood from his face wound changes between shots.

Towards the end of the film: Killmonger is about to kill Shuri at the top of the mine shaft and Shuri is backing up. Her elbow goes over the edge, but in the next shot which is from over Killmonger's shoulder looking down at her, she is at least a foot away from the edge.

When M'Baku challenges T'Challa, the decorations near his neck are in a different position between him facing the crowd, and him turning to face T'Challa.

Marvel Studios

At the start of the movie Black Panther gets shoes that are silent when he runs. Half way through the movie when he runs up the spiral ramp you can hear his footsteps. (01:00:00 - 01:01:00)

When Ross is interrogating Klaue, there's a shot from behind him and we can see the bug on his left shoulder. When he leaves the room and talks to T'Challa, the bug has vanished, but re-appears again shortly afterwards.

Marvel Studios

While T'Challa is fighting in his first challenge, the sun changes between shots.

When Killmonger cuts a woman's throat, in one shot a spear is not red, but in the very next shot it is.

During the mid-credits scene T'Challa is addressing the United Nations about Wakanda's true nature. A Welsh flag can be seen among the other nation's flags, which would suggest that Wales is a separate nation from The United Kingdom - not the case.

Marvel Studios

BLACK PANTHER TRIVIA

The Winter Soldier makes a cameo in a post credit scene.

Stan Lee does his Marvel cameo and can be seen taking Chadwick Boseman's winnings/chips at the casino saying "I will take these!"

Killmonger throws T'Challa down the waterfall. He does the same thing in the comics.

The way Black Panther takes down the rhino is exactly the same way he does in the comics.

Wakanda is shown on the map as where Southern Sudan is.

John Kani plays T'Chaka as an old man, while his son Atandwa Kani plays T'Chaka in his youth.

Michael B. Jordan kept to himself during filming, to reflect Killmonger's relationship with the other characters.

During the first few days of filming on the waterfall set, many of the actors and extras began to have difficulty keeping their eyes open, and began experiencing pain, irritation and discomfort. The crew at first suspected there was too much chlorine being used in the water, but they eventually realised what was actually going on... it was so bright on set due to light reflecting off the water, everyone's eyeballs were getting sunburned. The studio then had to buy sunglasses for everyone to wear in-between shots.

"Wakanda" comes from the Kenyan Wakamba (or Kamba) tribe.

Wesley Snipes attempted to get a "Black Panther" movie made in the 90's. After issues finding a director and suitable script, as well as facing other hurdles with effects and costume design, he abandoned the project, and eventually pursued another Marvel character - Blade, which ended up turning into a popular film trilogy.

Martin Freeman was asked how he felt being one of the few white actors and replied "You think, 'Right, this is what black actors feel like all the time.'"

There is a mid credit scene that shows T'Challa speaking about Wakanda in Vienna.

ANT-MAN AND THE WASP MISTAKES

Throughout the movie, Hank's lab in its shrunken form is constantly jostled and tossed around, but when it's restored to full size in a new location, nothing is out of place and everything still works perfectly.

As the ghost attacks Wasp in the hotel lobby, there's a guy unconscious in front of the piano who's there in some shots and missing in others.

At the school, when Scott's suit is malfunctioning and he's big in the janitor's closet, his head is tilted towards his right shoulder. When Hope is working on the suit, we see Scott's head is now tilted towards his left shoulder, even though he's stuck and wouldn't have been able to move around like that. But in the next shot it's back to his right.

While Hope is talking with Burch at the restaurant the bag of money and the device are on the table but in the next shot the device is now on the seat.

The outside of Hank's lab changes in different shots - sometimes there's a "no entry" sign inside a window on the right, other times it's missing. When Scott and Hope arrive there's a red logo on the door which is missing later. And when the ghost exits there's a "private property" notice beside the door which isn't there at other times.

When Susan goes to visit Burch and enters the building, she has the suitcase in her right hand but in the next shot she has it in her left hand. (00:21:45)

At the start when Hope is playing in her room, in a wide shot there's a wooden stand with a plant on it by the teddy bear in the background. In a closeup of her this stand has vanished.

Walt Disney Pictures

When the shrunken car is surrounded by pigeons, it's an all-glass roof, or black. When the shrunken car drives through a pipe later, its roof is silver. It changes back and forth again, just before/after Hank shrinks it.

Walt Disney Pictures

ANT-MAN AND THE WASP TRIVIA

While Bill Foster, played by Laurence Fishburne, is teaching the class, the words "Matrix" can be seen on the blackboard behind him, referring to the film series Laurence Fishburne starred in.

Paul Rudd actually learned the sleight-of-hand magic tricks he performs in the film - it's not special effects as one might assume.

Two of the actors in this film also have roles in the MCU's rival DC Extended Universe. Laurence Fishburne (Bill Foster) played Perry White in "Man of Steel" and "Batman V Superman," and Randall Park (Agent Woo) played Dr. Shin in "Aquaman."

The release date of this movie in the United States was July 6, 2018 whilst the release date in the United Kingdom was August 2, 2018 almost four weeks later. This marks the first time a Marvel Cinematic Universe movie has been released in the United Kingdom later than the United States. Every other MCU movie has either been released in the UK and USA the same week or released in the UK a week before the USA. The belief was that while the World Cup was on, the audience for the movie would be otherwise distracted, affecting the box office take.

Stan Lee makes his usual cameo as the guy that accidentally gets his car shrunk by Hope during the climactic chase. Sadly, this was the last Stan Lee cameo released before his death in November, 2018. (Although he had already filmed cameos for several other upcoming films before his death).

There is a post credit scene.

Casey said that she would like to get to shrink and help people. In the comics she was a member of the Young Avengers.

There is a mid credit scene linked to Avengers: Infinity War.

The film the trio are watching on the laptop while shrunken is "Them!" A 1954 film about giant ants attacking. It was the first "big bug" film of the 50s.

During the flashbacks when we see the younger Bill Foster, the character is not played by a digitally de-aged Laurence Fishburne as most would assume. For these brief scenes, the character is actually played by Laurence's son Langston. (Albeit made up to more closely resemble his father).

The song played throughout the film "C'mon, Get Happy" was the theme song from the 70s TV series "The Partridge Family." While Scott is lip syncing the words to the song he is imitating the late David Cassidy, the lead singer of the "Partridge Family."

One of the film's writers has slyly suggested that in his opinion, Norman Osbourne (aka, the Green Goblin of "Spider-Man" fame) is an associate of Sonny Burch, and is the one who wants the Quantum Technology.

The ghost was introduced in Iron Man #219 from 1987.

"Ant-Man and the Wasp" is the twentieth entry in the Marvel Cinematic Universe. Originally, "Captain Marvel" was meant to be released first, but their release dates were swapped. It is the second MCU sequel to be filmed in the wider 2.39:1 aspect ratio after the first film was shot in taller 1.85:1 ratio. (The other films being "The Avengers/Avengers: Age of Ultron"). Walton Goggins and Hannah John-Kamen, who play the villains in this film, both appeared in the 2018 "Tomb Raider" film, which was released just a few months prior to this. And the first publicity photo of the Wasp was released on what would have been the 100th birthday of Jack Kirby - the character's co-creator.

CAPTAIN MARVEL MISTAKES

Carol Danvers' name appears on her dog tags as "Carol Danvers," but US military dog tags list the surname first, then given name. E.g. "Danvers, Carol."

As Vers is about to punch the person dressed like the Skrull, a woman in a flowery pantsuit is visible in the background, behind him. Next shot and she is walking behind Vers making a rather conspicuous horrified facepalm, and coming from the wrong direction. (00:33:50)

The internet cafe Vers visits runs a piece of software even more cutting edge than the brand new, still beta version of Windows 95; Netscape Navigator 4, a release from 1997 - certainly not 1995, when it still had very squared highly recognizable buttons and icons of a different color than those portrayed here. (00:35:15)

When Minerva mistakenly picks up a NERF gun to shoot Carol, the blaster she picks up is a Sharpshooter II, released in 1995. The occupants of the station were supposed to have been stranded there for six years and could not logically have obtained this item.

In the internet cafe, Vers searches for the name of the bar conveniently seen on the piece of machinery conveniently dropped by the Skrull. She can't google it, being 1995, so she uses Altavista. Props to the prop department for using the original logo of Altavista, but the URL appearing as result for the search is http://www.altavista.com/search etc, while it should have been http://www.altavista.digital.com, since Altavista in its early years did not own the altavista.com domain name.

Coming out of the train, Vers moves through the crowd. She passes by the same person with a petrol windbreaker, reading a newspaper. She moves past him but he's still in front of her in the next shot.(00:33:40)

The movie is set in June 1995, based on the calendar at Rambeau's house, but some of the movies on the shelf at Blockbuster weren't released yet, like First Knight which only opened in theaters in July 1995, and wasn't released on VHS until in December. (00:24:00)

The red songbook on Rambeau's piano is Cajun and Zydeco Classics, first published in 2005, ten years after this scene is supposed to have taken place. (01:20:00)

Everyone is gathered in front of Maria's computer waiting for the audio CD to load. Maria's computer is actually from the future, since it has installed not Windows 95 (beta or not) like in the internet cafe, but Windows ME or 2000 (telltale detail; the icon of the recycle bin). (01:05:45)

Vers saves Fury, blowing a hole in the ceiling and somehow getting to the upper floor (why she does not blast holes for the remaining floors as well is unclear). They should be then at -4 from the -5 they were in, but they are shown ascending a flight of stairs, at the top of which Coulson lets them enter the door for level -4.

When Vers is using the payphone across from Blockbuster, the phone says it costs 25 cents for a call, but down below there is a big notice on the phone saying effective Nov. 1, 1995 the rate is going up to 25 cents. Trouble is it is June 1995, still five months before the rate change, and yet it already costs 25 cents.

(00:25:40)

When Nick Fury types 'The Protector Initiative', that's a newer keyboard than the setting. The F11 function key has a second feature, which wasn't added until later. (01:51:15)

The calendar on the wall behind Fury when they are listening to the audio at Rambeau's house correctly lists the days for June 1995 (1st is a Thursday and 30th is a Friday), but the days for May and July are wrong (it shows May 1st on Sunday and last day as 30th on Tuesday, but 1st was Monday, and May has 31 days, not 30. It shows July 1st as Wednesday when it was actually Saturday, and the month of July only having 28 days). (01:05:00)

In her second encounter with the Supreme Intelligence, Carol's memories 'jogged' by the Earth's sojourn include a record of "Come as you are" by Nirvana. A memory that Carol couldn't possibly have, having become Vers in 1989, and with the song being part of Nirvana's ultra-famous "Nevermind" album which came out in 1991. (01:27:30)

One blast of the stun weapon by the Skrulls is all it takes to KO Carol long enough to be kidnapped, taken aboard the ship and brain probed, but in the fight scene that ensues she gets hit multiple times and just shrugs it off like it's nothing.

Vers KOs the Skrull she does the warcry thing at, and then another one on the corridor steps. She is then seen fighting from the perspective of the corridor to her right, but there are no Skrulls in sight against that door, while at least one was already lying down there. There are two when the camera gets back closer, and when she neutralizes the last one who bounces onto his own stun mace, there are again two, and she somehow got between the last one and the others. (00:20:30)

Walt Disney Pictures

When Vers 'proves' to Fury she's not a Skrull by photon blast usage, Brie Larson's hand is either under her chin or on the table; it makes no difference for the reverse shots that stay always the same. (00:41:00)

When Vers arrives at the bar, Nick Fury is already there. She went straight to the bar after stealing the bike, while Fury needed still to learn about the theft, link it to the case, with investigations taking place to maybe (only possibility that would not depend on the vehicle being reported) figure out that Pancho's was the destination from examining the search history of the browser. Fury went there by car. His boss also explicitly says to work on the case alone. Amazing he could be there with such timing.

Monica is showing Carol some photos from the past. The first one is a Halloween one; you can see in the wide shot how her two hands move together on the corner of the picture, but in the close-up she is holding it on both opposite sides. (01:01:15)

After taking the motorcycle, Danvers rides to the bar and passes a blue and white open-bed Ford pickup. There are two things wrong with the truck's license plate: it is a non-commercial California plate "1TAH285" (pickups in California back then had to have commercial plates, form 1A23456, unless a special allowance was made if they always have a camper), and the plate is blue on white which was first used with plates starting with "2." A plate of form 1ABC234 starting with "1" is gold on blue. (00:38:00)

CAPTAIN MARVEL TRIVIA

The first Marvel film released after Stan Lee's death. In tribute, the usual opening ident, which has the comic book characters in the Marvel Studios logo, instead shows multiple images of Stan Lee.

When Captain Marvel strides out of the store, she goes over to a security guard in his car parked nearby. This guard is played by real-life Marvel security director Barry Curtis.

Brie Larson is actually allergic to cats, so when filming with Goose the real cat had to be replaced by a puppet or with CGI.

In the Blockbuster, Danvers blasts a standee of True Lies. The directors' first choice of standee was actually The Mask (which makes sense, being a green-skinned character who she'd rightly think was a Skrull and attack), but New Line Cinema refused to allow it.

While we never find out in the movie who Yon-Rogg saw when he visited the Supreme Intelligence, being "the person he admires above all", a deleted scene gives the answer...himself.

Kelly Sue Deconnick, notable writer of Captain Marvel comics, makes a cameo on the train where Vers is looking for the Skrulls.

This film portrays the Kree Supreme Intelligence as an abstract form that takes the appearance of a person familiar to whomever is conversing with it. In the comics, the Supreme Intelligence does have an identifiable form: a floating green head somewhat resembling Jabba the Hutt with glowing yellow eyes and tentacles.

Captain Marvel's name is never spoken in the film. It is only mentioned in the closing credits.

The movie was released on March 8th 2019, International Women's Day.

Stan Lee's cameo actually references another cameo he made as himself, in 1995's Mallrats - he's reading the script for that on the train. This marks the first time he's explicitly himself in a Marvel Cinematic Universe film (he identified himself as Stan Lee in Fantastic 4: Rise of the Silver Surfer), not just a random character. In fact Guardians of the Galaxy, Vol. 2 confirms he's actually playing the same character in every cameo, a Watcher Informant, roaming the multiverse and reporting back his discoveries. And given he's reading the Mallrats script here, that means Stan Lee himself was actually an alien being all along, observing humanity and others. And of course that means the real Stan Lee exists in the MCU, so created comics based on characters who really exist, albeit maybe in another universe...but you could go on like that forever.

Walt Disney Pictures

Chris Evans' appearance in this film's post-credit sequence marks the tenth time he has portrayed Captain America, surpassing Hugh Jackman for the record of playing the same comic book character in the most films. Evans would add on to his own record a few weeks later by appearing in "Avengers: Endgame."

Make sure to stay for two extra scenes during and after the credits.

In the comics, Carol's cat is called Chewie, a reference to Star Wars. Intended as a nostalgic reference (the comics originating before the Star Wars prequels and later movies), it was changed to Goose (from Top Gun) for this movie, because Star Wars movies are still ongoing, making Chewie too "current."

AVENGERS: ENDGAME MISTAKES

In the final battle, Wasp and Ant-Man are in the van trying to get the quantum tunnel operational. We cut back to the fight and we can see Ant-Man there too, fighting in his giant form. (02:22:20 - 02:23:00)

When Thanos is being questioned about where the stones are, Captain Marvel has her arm wrapped around his neck in a head-lock and War Machine is holding onto his right arm. Just as Bruce goes to push Thanos over, both Captain Marvel and War Machine suddenly do not have their hands on him. There is no reason that they would have let go of him. Nor would there have been enough time for them to let go of him in between shots. (00:18:10)

While Hulk eats breakfast with Cap, Nat and Scott, the crepe on the top is cut in two. In the next shot it's in one piece, then in two again. (00:38:30)

Marvel Studios

When the camera is panning over the entire army on the Avengers' side for the first time, Captain America is standing in front of everyone, and his shield is intact and round again, while Thanos broke it earlier. The next time we see it, it's back to being broken.

New Asgard is in Tonsberg, Norway, but was filmed in Scotland. The truck Hulk and Rocket use to get there has a UK licence plate (SW61 5PN), whereas Norwegian plates use two letters followed by 4 or 5 numbers. Plus the pizza boxes in Thor's house have a phone number in UK format (01632 960776) not Norwegian. In fact, the 01632 area code is specifically designated for fictional use in the UK. Norwegian telephone numbers use fewer digits. (00:48:50)

When the Ancient One is explaining to Bruce that taking the Time Stone will affect their reality, there is a shot from behind the Ancient One where she says "Millions will suffer", but her mouth doesn't move when she says the line. (01:24:20)

When Thanos gets the Iron Gauntlet, he has armour on his right arm. When he fights Captain Marvel, the piece of armour disappears from one shot to another so his arms are free to put on the Gauntlet. (02:28:45)

When the Avengers are discussing where Thanos might be, Steve tells Tony that he fought him. In the shot where Tony says "Who told you that", his right hand is holding onto the robe he is wearing. The camera changes angles and his right hand is now shown touching the table. It then cuts back to Tony, where his right hand is touching the robe again. (00:10:39)

When Tony takes off the Nano Arc Reactor and places it on Steve's hand, he drops to the ground. Captain Marvel is shown in the back of shot, raising her hands slightly as if she is preparing to catch him. It then cuts to a wide shot where her hands are suddenly at ease. (00:12:15)

Scott arrives in the park and sees hundreds of memorials listing people who were killed by Thanos. In the first close-up shot shown of one of the memorials, the name Norbert Lamey can be seen five rows from the top on the right hand side. The camera then pans to Scott walking in front of the memorial to the right of it. The name Norbert Lamey can be seen repeated on the opposite side of the memorial Scott stands in front of. (00:24:25)

In the first Avengers film Steve lost his helmet after the battle and got dirty, with a damaged suit and battered face, but here while they are arresting Loki he has the helmet on and the suit is intact and clean. Can't be that he cleaned himself up, because in the Avengers post-credit scene eating shawarma (after arresting Loki), Cap's suit is still dirty from the battle. Can't be that he got changed before heading down (and why would he?) because in the shawarma scene from the first Avengers movie he's still in his damaged/dirty suit after everything.

When the Avengers return from the quantum tunnel with the stones, their order is Hulk, Tony, Steve, Clint. But seconds later this changes to Hulk, Steve, Clint then Tony. (01:55:18)

When Steve starts fighting 2012 Steve, he places the case containing Loki's sceptre on the ground. He then starts to run towards 2012 Steve, leaving the case far behind him. The two then start fighting hand to hand, and the case is suddenly right beside them. (01:22:30)

Marvel Studios

When Tony begins to walk back to his house carrying his daughter, he is holding the Iron Man helmet he made for Pepper, the top of it. In the next shot, he is suddenly holding the side of the helmet. (00:33:55)

At the end of the movie, when Thor is speaking with Valkyrie about being the new Queen of Asgard, his beard is trimmed and much shorter. In the next scene aboard the ship with the Guardians when he and Quill are arguing about who is in charge, Thor's beard is back to how long it was earlier in the film. (02:40:20 - 02:41:45)

When the Ancient One is showing Bruce the flow of time, a projection of the Infinity Stones are shown rotating around the flow of time she projects. Just as Bruce says "Because once we're done with the stones...", the projection of the Space Stone is shown rotating away from Bruce and more towards the Ancient One. The camera changes angles, and the Space Stone is now closer to Bruce, and is shown rotating past the same area it did in the previous shot. (01:24:30)

In the Hulk scene at the diner, once Scott takes the picture of the kids, in the frontal shots he is holding the phone with his right hand and hands it to them, while the reverse shots don't match - egregiously noticeable when he says "I don't want a picture with them" waving an empty right hand. (00:38:05)

Marvel Studios

When Scott is explaining the Quantum Realm to Steve and Nat, he begins eating a sandwich that he is holding in his right hand. It then cuts to a different angle where the sandwich is in his left hand. (00:32:00)

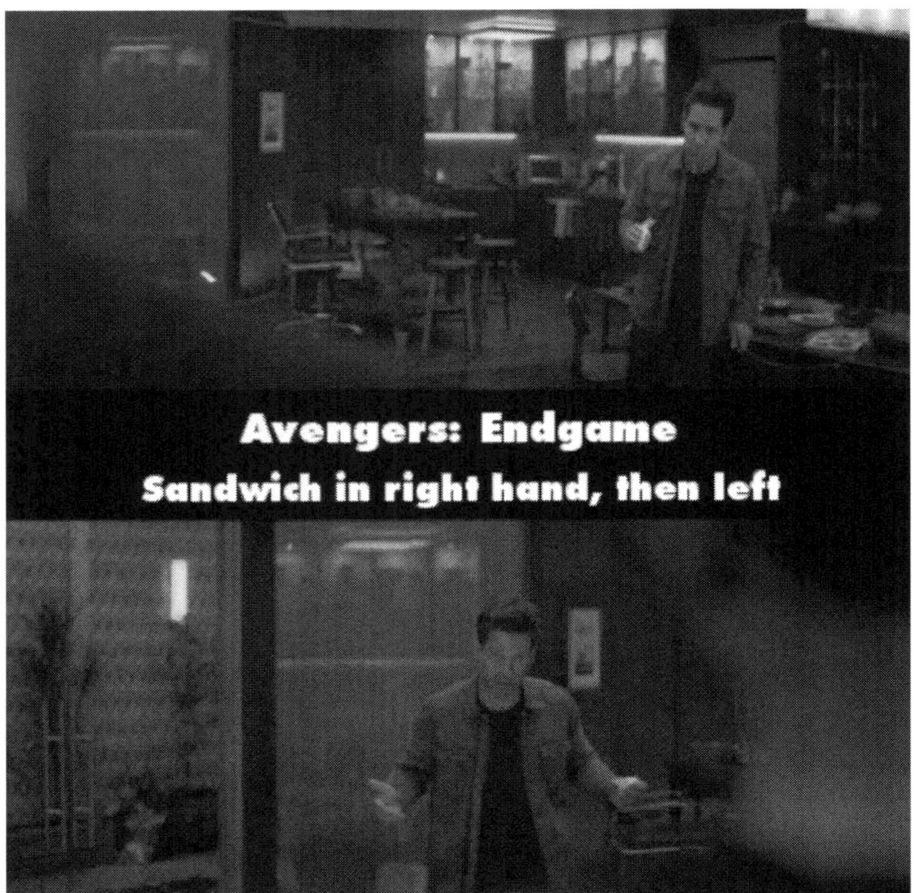

Marvel Studios

When Bruce hands the phone over to Scott so that he can take his photo with the three kids, Scott takes the phone and initially holds it with two hands. It then cuts to a wide shot of Scott beginning to stand, where the phone is now only in his right hand. (00:37:55)

While the Avengers are standing on the time machine just before the time heist, Barton promises Rocket he will bring back the ship in one piece. Rocket then says "as promises go, that was pretty lame", and has his arms folded when he says this. It then cuts to a shot of the group, and Rocket's arms are suddenly by his side.(01:06:35)

AVENGERS: ENDGAME TRIVIA

In the comics Falcon has taken on the mantle of Captain America before.

Robert Downey Jr. was the only member of the cast who was allowed to read the entire script.

A young man is shown on screen towards the end with the others, and it's not immediately obvious who it is - it's Harley Keener, played by Ty Simpkins, the boy in Iron Man 3.

The man talking to Cap at the support group about his date is Joe Russo, one of the directors of the movie.

Thanos' gauntlet bears a striking resemblance to the relic of the hand of St. Teresa de Jesus, one of the most important holy relics in Spain.

Marvel Studios

During the Steve Rogers support group scene, the bald man with glasses and goatee is none other than Jim Starlin, the comics writer and artist who created Thanos.

Marvel Studios

Stan Lee makes his last cameo as the hippie that yells at the army in 1970.

The scene with Steve on the elevator with the agents of Shield (Hydra) is a callback to The Winter Soldier, with the obvious flip that this time he deceives them and avoids a fight.

The arc reactor that says "Proof that Tony Stark has a heart" is the gift Pepper made for Tony in Iron Man 1 after she removed his old reactor.

One of the time-travel movies referenced by Ant-Man is "Hot Tub Time Machine", which featured Sebastian Stan, who plays Bucky in the MCU. In fact several of the films or franchises mentioned during the scene feature MCU stars. "Star Trek" had Chris Hemsworth in a small role in the 2009 film (If Inhumans still counts as MCU, then Anson Mount has been on Star Trek Discovery). Scott mentions 'Die Hard, ' which had Samuel L. Jackson in the third film. Interestingly, they don't mention Doctor Who, which has featured myriad MCU actors over the years, including Karen Gillan (Nebula), Christopher Eccleston (Malaketh the Dark Elf), and David Tenant (The Purple Man).

Spoiler! Falcon announces his arrival to Captain America with "on your left", the same phrase Cap taunted him with when they first met in Winter Soldier.

When Wasp appears to join the final battle, look to her right and you can see the Ravagers from Guardians of the Galaxy, including Kraglin (Sean Gunn), and even Howard the Duck.

The youngest son of Clint's middle name is Pietro, after Pietro Maximoff, the brother of Scarlet Witch.

Near the start, Okoye submits a report about an earthquake in the Atlantic, saying they should leave it alone. This is a potential tease for Namor the Sub-Mariner, ruler of Atlantis. This has been hinted at before, with a map in Iron Man 2 showing a point of interest in the Atlantic - the same map which flagged up Wakanda long before the official introduction of Black Panther.

Spoilers: Captain America being worthy of lifting Thor's hammer Mjölnir is something that is pulled from the pages of the comics directly, most notably in this context the Civil War comics. He'd previously been able to move it fractionally in Age of Ultron - Joss Whedon has implied he was able to lift it the whole time, just pretended he couldn't so as to spare Thor's feelings.

Ken Jeong and Yvette Nicole Brown have cameos in the film. The two co-starred in the TV sitcom "Community," which "Endgame" directors Joe and Anthony Russo both worked on.

The number on Scott Lang's storage unit is 616. This is the same number used to refer to Earth Prime (the primary Earth 'continuity') in Marvel comics.

Before the last battle Steve says "Avengers Assemble," a classic line from the comics which despite a few teases hadn't yet been said in the MCU.

Despite her prominent billing, Brie Larson has only 10 minutes of screen time.

Spoiler! After Tony snaps his fingers at the end, a scene was filmed with him having a vision of his daughter Morgan, now grown up, played by 13 Reasons Why star Katherine Langford. Much like Thanos' conversation with a young Gamora in Infinity War, Tony and Morgan would discuss what he'd just done and she'd forgive him, putting him at peace. The scene was ultimately scrapped because there wasn't the emotional connection with an adult version of his daughter, and the Russos dismissed it as "too many ideas in an overly complicated movie."

SPIDER-MAN: FAR FROM HOME MISTAKES

When Peter and MJ hug on Tower Bridge he gets some blood from his face onto the left shoulder of her jacket. From other angles there's no blood.

In the (phony) bar, Peter's straw goes from bendy to straight to bendy to straight in different shots.

When Happy is talking to Peter in the kitchen at the charity event, from the angle over Happy's shoulder he's talking but the side of his face isn't moving, from that angle we should see his chin move up and down.

After Spidey fights with Beck for the first time he gets a wound on his right cheekbone which is fresh, then dry, then fresh again.

When Beck and Peter are talking together on top of a building, their heads change positions several times between shots. From looking at each other to straight ahead and every other direction.

The German woman screams "Nacht Monkey" when Peter jumps off the train, but the German for "Night Monkey" is "Nachtaffe".

When Peter is in a Dutch cell, he is surrounded by Dutchmen who greet him in Dutch at first. Then Peter breaks out of the cell, the Dutch guard hears the lock break and yells to his fellow countrymen "is everything OK with you guys?" instead of yelling it in Dutch. (01:20:00 - 01:20:30)

SPIDER-MAN: FAR FROM HOME TRIVIA

Samuel Jackson spotted that the eye patch his character wears in the movie switched eyes in the promotional posters announcing the movie in Los Angeles.

Marvel Studios

Peter's passport has his birthday as 10th August. That's the date Amazing Fantasy #15 was released, where Spider-Man made his debut appearance.

Spoilers! Back to form for MCU films after Endgame bucked the trend, there are two post credit sequences - one features JK Simmons as J Jonah Jameson, reprising his role from the Sam Raimi Spider-Man movies, only this time JJJ is a host for a conspiracy-fuelled website-based show. He airs footage from Mysterio outing Peter Parker as Spider-Man and framing him for the death of Mysterio and the carnage in London. The second reveals that Nick Fury and Maria Hill have actually been Skrulls the entire movie, standing in at the real Fury's request so he can take a simulated beach vacation in space...somewhere.

Backstage at the charity fundraiser, a poster can be seen featuring Crusher Hogan. Crusher Hogan was the wrestler faced by a masked Peter Parker faced in Spider-Man's first appearance in Amazing Fantasy #15.

The car driven by Nick Fury and Maria Hill has license plate MTU83779. This is a reference to Marvel Team Up #83 from July, 1979 titled "Spider-Man and Nick Fury."

When creating the new Spider-Man suit on the jet, Happy plays Back in Black by AC/DC, which is the same song that played while Tony Stark configured the first Iron Man suit.

Jake Gyllenhaal, who portrays Mysterio in this film, nearly took over the role of Spider-Man from Tobey Maguire for "Spider-Man 2" after Maguire suffered a back injury filming "Seabiscuit."

The big check has the logo of Synchrony Bank, which is the provider of official Marvel credit cards.

Peter's suitcase has the initials BFP: Benjamin Franklin Parker, Uncle Ben.

Quentin Beck says our earth is "dimension 616." In the comics,

Earth-616 is the "main" dimension the majority of Marvel comics are set in.

Flash says that he saw on the internet an article about Morris Bench, aka Hydro-Man from Marvel comics.

Beck talks about Earth-833, known in the comics as being the original universe of "Spider-UK." In the comics it was destroyed, as Beck claims happened to his world.

When May picks up Peter at the airport there is a car with the license plate AMF1562 - a reference to Amazing Fantasy #15 comic book from 1962.

The various elementals are homages to classic Spider-Man enemies Cyclone, Hydro-Man, Molten-Man, and Sandman.

Towards the end while Spidey swings around the city he passes by the same building where Harry Osborne lived in the Sam Raimi Spider-Man films.

Spider-Man: Far from Home is the first Spider-Man film to ever make over a billion dollars at the box office.

The red/black suit made by Peter resembles the one on the cover of Amazing Fantasy #15 from 1962.

While Ned takes a pic in Venice, in the background there is a boat with "ASM 212" on it, that's a reference to the Amazing Spider-man comic book #212 where the Hydro Man was introduced.

Despite Avengers: Endgame being viewed as the "finale" of the MCU to date, this is the official final movie of "Phase 3", as it's known. Producer Kevin Feige said: "As we were working on Endgame we realised that the true end of the entire Infinity Saga, the final film of Phase 3, had to be Spider-Man: Far From Home, because we lose Tony Stark at the end of Endgame. The relationship between Peter Parker and Tony Stark is so special."

The black suit was also seen in Spider-Man: Into the Spider-Verse.

THANK YOU

Thank you for reading! I hope you enjoyed it, and if so please tell your friends, share it, lend it...spread the word! Please leave a review on Amazon - if you like this, there's plenty more where this came from. And if you've got any observations of your own, please submit them to moviemistakes.com. I'd love to hear any suggestions, corrections, thoughts and opinions - please get in touch at jon@moviemistakes.com.

ABOUT THE AUTHOR

Jon Sandys

I cannot lie - I haven't spotted all of these myself. After all, I've only got one pair of eyes, and only one lifetime! They've been accumulated over the past 20 years from myself and thousands of other eagle-eyed fans across the world, and all stored on my website, moviemistakes.com. But rather than forcing you to trawl through the 100,000+ entries on the site, I thought it was worth selecting the cream of the crop for a book like this.

Back in September 1996, I was 17 years old, a huge film fan, and fairly computer obsessed. I wanted to make a web page, but couldn't really think of what to do. I eventually took a few continuity mistakes and film facts, put them into a website along with an e-mail address, and that was about it. Over time, thanks to word of mouth and the occasional bit of press, it's built into the collection it is today, covering movies, TV shows, even books and games, and including trivia, quotes and more.

This book is primarily designed to point you in the direction of all those little things that you may not have noticed the first, or second, or even third time around. It is for entertainment and educational purposes only. It should not prevent you from going go on with your life as normal. I take no responsibility when you're next watching something and catch yourself thinking 'I'm sure her sleeves were rolled up in the last shot...' But, if after reading it, you no longer can watch things without picking them apart for the most minute mistakes, I'm afraid there's only one piece of advice I can give you...you'll always find a home with similarly afflicted people at moviemistakes.com.

BOOKS BY THIS AUTHOR

Great Movie Mistakes

Have you seen the stormtrooper banging his head in Star Wars?

Did you notice the gas canister in the chariot in Gladiator?

How about the missing Spitfire engine in Dunkirk?

How did the flyers get into the vault in Ocean's 11?

How does Harry Potter change his T-shirt in his sleep?

Who's the guy with sunglasses and a cowboy hat in the background of Pirates of the Caribbean?

This book collects over 500 great movie mistakes together, 80 with images so you can see them for yourself, and many with the time they occur, making them easier to find in your own copy. Bloopers throughout movie history, from Snow White and the Seven Dwarfs through to Star Wars: The Last Jedi. From continuity mistakes to crewmembers in shot to historical errors, over 8 decades, you'll be amazed what you've missed in some of your favourite movies.

Great Movie Trivia

Over 700 pieces of trivia from movies old and new, many with pictures identifying the scene in question so you know what or who to look out for. From Gone with the Wind to Black Panther, there'll be something you didn't know about all your favourite movies:

* In Frozen, when Anna is outside the gates during 'For The First Time in Forever', you can see the backs of Flynn and Rapunzel from 'Tangled'.

* According to the Guinness Book of Records, the Lord of the Rings holds the record for the greatest number of false feet used in one movie: 60,000.

* The 'oil' that was used to lubricate the Tin Man in The Wizard of Oz was not really oil. It was discovered that oil would not photograph well, so they used chocolate syrup instead.

* Wes Craven named A Nightmare on Elm Street's Freddy Krueger after a bully who tortured him in school.

Great Tv Mistakes

500 mistakes from 50 fan-favourite TV shows, many with pictures. From the infamous coffee cup in Game of Thrones to impossible triplets in the Golden Girls, crewmembers in shot, characters' names changing, visible boom microphones, plot holes and continuity errors galore. Slipups in 24, Brooklyn Nine-Nine, Charmed, Dexter, Doctor Who, Frasier, King of the Hill, Lost, M*A*S*H, The Office, Red Dwarf, Sex and the City, The Simpsons, Star Trek, Supernatural, The West Wing, The X-Files and many more. You'll be amazed what you've missed in some of your favourite shows!

Printed in Great Britain
by Amazon

67302160R00123